315 OVER A BEER

www.mascotbooks.com

315 Over a Beer: Leadership Conversations with an Old Salt for Junior Officers

©2025 Erik R. Nilsson. All Rights Reserved. No part of this publication may be reproduced, stored in a retrieval system or transmitted in any form by any means electronic, mechanical, or photocopying, recording or otherwise without the permission of the author.

The author has tried to recreate events, locales, and conversations from their memories of them. In order to maintain their anonymity in some instances, the author has changed the names of individuals and places, and may have changed some identifying characteristics and details such as physical properties, occupations, and places of residence.

The views expressed in this publication are those of the author and do not necessarily reflect the official policy or position of the Department of Defense or the U.S. government. The public release clearance of this publication by the Department of Defense does not imply Department of Defense endorsement or factual accuracy of the material.

For more information, please contact:
Mascot Books, an imprint of Amplify Publishing Group
620 Herndon Parkway, Suite 220
Herndon, VA 20170
info@mascotbooks.com

Library of Congress Control Number: 2024923429

CPSIA Code: PRV1224A

ISBN-13: 979-8-89138-295-4

Printed in the United States

For my wife, Alison, for everything;
and for my sons, Jake and Chase,
leaders in their own rights.

Barracks Room 315

315 OVER *a* BEER

Leadership Conversations *with* an Old Salt *for* Junior Officers

ERIK R. NILSSON
CAPTAIN, U.S. NAVY (RET.)

Contents

INTRODUCTION ix

1. PERSPECTIVE 1

2. A DEFINITION OF LEADERSHIP 7

3. THE ARTIST'S TOOLBOX 11

4. FIRST AND FOREMOST 13

5. "ENSIGNS SHOULD BE SEEN AND NOT HEARD" 17

6. RIGHT THE SHIP 21

7. CREDIBILITY 27

8. LIBERTY AND ACCOUNTABILITY 31

9. BUILDING RELATIONSHIPS 43

10. GATOR 47

11. FAIR IN THE CHANNEL 53

12. NAVY CULTURE—THE NAVY IS NOT VMI 63

13. RAPID-FIRE MEMES 69

14. A FEW WORDS OF CAUTION 79

15. ADVICE FOR WORKING WITH SENIOR LEADERS 95

16.	THE DAY-TO-DAY GRIND	99
17.	DESIGNATED DRIVER	101
18.	BEST PRACTICES	111
19.	WHITEBOARD'ISMS	117
20.	YOUR PHILOSOPHY	119
21.	LEARNING IS A NEVER-ENDING PROCESS	125
22.	A GENERATIONAL PERSPECTIVE	127
	ABOUT THE AUTHOR	131

Introduction

This short book started out as a brainstorming effort to collect ideas and topics that I was putting together to make a "podcast" for my son and his barracks roommates at the Virginia Military Institute (VMI)—barracks room number 315. I envisioned a conversation over a beer about VMI, leadership, and a sea story or two. The podcast took off and had a fairly wide listening audience throughout the barracks, a minor success. To be clear, though, the podcasts were recorded voice notes that I uploaded to a shared drive. When the Cadets went home for the summer, the podcast petered off. I never picked it back up when the new year started; I just ran out of time with my job. Later, I was invited to speak at VMI for a Navy training event, and much of what I talked about came from the podcasts. I realized that there was a demand for the content, and I decided to commit the collection of ideas and stories to paper.

I intended for this book to be a graduation gift to my son and his roommates—a limited edition, so to speak—and get a few copies made at the local print shop. It turned out that more people were interested than I anticipated, so I decided to try to get the book published. Good leadership and management are universal; in this book, I offer a perspective on both, and there is potential to apply the tenets and ideas across many disciplines. To reach that broader audience, and because VMI is a niche audience, I've added footnotes in some places and taken the liberty to offer context in other places where the VMI and military jargon need to be explained.

I enjoy telling stories. This book is mostly a collection of stories that capture the lessons I learned as a junior officer, or "JO," during my first few years in the Navy, and with these stories I want to both teach and entertain. I offer you the opportunity to learn from my mistakes, gain a few leadership and management tools, and get a glimpse into the version of the Navy in which your leaders grew up. I recognize that it is a different navy now, and, in most respects, we have evolved into a much more lethal force. But lessons on the art of leadership, management tools, relationship-building, credibility, and what it means to be a JO are timeless.

I hope you enjoy this book and learn from it.

1

Perspective

Your perspective is your reality. Perspective is important—it anchors your worldview. But when an anchor is holding a ship at anchorage, the ship can swing on the anchor depending on the seas and winds, and it can even drag off the anchorage if it does not hold. If you need or want to shift your anchorage, you can heave around, take it up, and move to a better spot. Like an anchorage, you can change your perspective based on the information you are taking in around you. It is a continuous process of taking in information, assessing that information, and making decisions based on the inputs.

Just before graduation week at VMI, a good friend and I were sitting on a hillside drinking beer during a NROTC* seniors' party at our instructor's farm. We matter-of-factly decided he would be CNO and I would be VCNO.† Lofty goals for one of the top grads and number eleven out of eleven in our class of newly commissioning Ensigns. You see, there was never

---

* Naval Reserve Officers Training Corps
† Chief of Naval Operations and Vice Chief of Naval Operations

any doubt about how far we *could* go—VMI helped to develop that belief in us—it only mattered how far we *wanted* to go.

I graduated from VMI in 1993, when the military was downsizing during the Clinton-era cuts. I did not attend VMI on a scholarship, so I had to compete for my commission into the Navy. You might say I am a true volunteer; I paid to go to VMI and I wanted the commission—it was not a debt to be paid off. But as much as I wanted to be a naval officer, my transition from VMI Cadet to U.S. Navy Surface Warfare Officer (SWO) Ensign was not smooth.

The author and his father, Commissioning, May 1993

I struggled to find my place in the wardroom* of my first ship—a relatively new WHIDBEY ISLAND-class amphibious

---

*   The officers eat in the wardroom; the Chief Petty Officers eat in the CPO mess; and the enlisted Sailors eat on the mess decks. Concurrently, the officers as a collective are commonly called "the wardroom," and the Chiefs are referred to as "the Chief's mess."

warship. I didn't fit in, and I really didn't care. I knocked out all my qualifications ("quals" for short) quickly, but my attitude did not play well with my department heads or my second commanding officer. We had twenty-four months to qualify as a Surface Warfare Officer—I knocked out all my quals* in about eight months, and I finally got my board at the twenty-three-month, three-week, five-day mark. The board was brutal, and I was not supposed to pass, but my new department head went to bat for me. After five miserable hours, I passed the board. I made an angry decision later that evening to resign my commission and seek other employment (obviously, I changed my mind). Why I stayed I will get to later, but at this point, I regretted my decision to even come into the Navy. I was bitter to say the least. This was not what I expected, not how I wanted to be treated, and it did not feel professional.

It would be easy to say that I had no mentors or guidance during those first couple of years—but it would also be a lie. I had some fantastic mentors; I just didn't recognize it at the time. My first commanding officer was the coolest SWO ever—a man who taught and made his expectations clear. The first Executive Officer was patient and instructive. The Chief Petty Officers' mess was awesome and took me under their wing. The ship's Mustangs—Limited Duty Officers and Chief Warrant Officers— were a constant source of support and advice and still are today. And I had a couple of close friends who had similar feelings, and

---

* Both enlisted personnel and officers are assigned to complete a Personal Qualifications Standards (PQS) for a watch station or a job to demonstrate a required level of proficiency and understanding of the position. There are certain observed tasks and usually a written and/or oral exam to complete the process.

we tended to commiserate over a few beers. But in the wardroom, I was a round peg in a square hole, and I hated that feeling.

What I did love, though, was to drive the ship and work with my Sailors.

Just prior to our deployment workups (fleet-training exercises), we had a visit from the Surface Community Detailers, the folks that work with us to find jobs within the Navy. We were directed to sign up for a time slot with the senior detailer. I did not sign up out of petulance or insolence; I sincerely did not want to waste the man's time. I went to the wardroom for a cup of coffee and ran into the senior detailer. I was on his list, and he asked why I failed to sign up. I told him that I was getting out, didn't want to waste his time, and declined the interview. The O-6* insisted, so being an obedient O-2, I sat down. After some discussion, he got to the question, "How would you like to be the navigator on a shooter overseas?" I replied that I'd consider it. He said, "Good, we have an agreement then."

I said to him, "Sir, we didn't agree to anything. I said I'd consider it."

He looked at me and said, "Sure."

A few weeks later, the message came in that I was being offered the opportunity to go to Yokosuka, Japan, to be the navigator on an OLIVER HAZARD PERRY-class guided missile frigate (FFG). My department head at the time was the First Lieutenant; she was the boss of the entire deck department. She

---

* Naval officer ranks are known by their noun names as well as alphanumeric designators: Ensign (O-1), Lieutenant Junior Grade (O-2), Lieutenant (O-3), Lieutenant Commander (O-4), Commander (O-5), Captain (O-6), Rear Admiral (Lower Half) (O-7), Rear Admiral (O-8), Vice Admiral (O-9), and Admiral (O-10). This man significantly outranked me.

was previously stationed in Yokosuka, so she sat me down and said, "Erik, you are a diamond in the rough. You would much rather be in the cockpit of a PT boat with your dog tags flying in the wind and your arms around your Sailors. That FFG will be your PT boat. You need a fresh start; take the job." I did, and I loved it. I learned from my mistakes and continued to be surrounded by mentors and leaders who I learned from and listened to, and that experience launched me into my career as a SWO.

Your career will have ups and downs. Some days it will be exhilarating and awesome, and some days it will just plain suck. I am not too sure when I really made the decision to stay, but I decided that I would stick around as long as I was challenged and was having fun. The two did not have to be mutually inclusive, but when they were both missing, it was time to go. I never hit that point. Your career is yours, and you should make it what you want. I made career choices based on what I wanted to do, but not always what I should have done as far as career progression. By choice, I never did a bureau or OPNAV* tour, so that limited my upward mobility, and I was okay with that. Aside from one tour, I always took operational jobs, and that was what I wanted. When I met my wife and we started a family, the decision process changed: the decisions were not mine alone; we made them together. There have been many sacrifices made along the way, but I think that makes us stronger and makes us appreciate what we have together. Having a family also made me more serious about my job. If I screwed up when I was single, it was just me. Now, I had my wife and kids to think about, too.

---

* The Bureau of Naval Personnel—now Navy Personnel Command—located in Millington, Tennessee, and the Office of the Chief of Naval Operations, located in Washington, DC, in the Pentagon.

I think I was successful, and my service reputation remains solid. But your standpoint now is exactly the same as where I started. I hope this short read will give you a jump start on what to consider as you develop your leadership style and help you manage the expectations you have set for yourself. You should also consider the leadership and mentoring you will receive and the expectations you set for your leaders. Your leaders may motivate you and give you the belief that you can accomplish anything, and some will disappoint the hell out of you and make you want to leave the Navy in disgust. But know this: the career path you set out for now and what you initially see in front of you will look completely different in twenty years when you look in the rearview mirror.

Now that I've left the formation to proceed with other duties and challenges, I can reflect on my past and look to the future. I truly believe that it is a great time to be a SWO—you will be faced with emerging opportunities and challenges. New classes of ships are coming online, technology is rapidly expanding our horizons and should be leveraged by the folks that understand it better than we old salts do, and for forever and a day, Sailors need and deserve fantastic leadership. The leadership style you develop and apply is absolutely critical to your success and that of your Sailors. When you look at your Sailors, you will see a reflection of yourself—for better or worse. Make it for the better. The clouds on the horizon portend conflict. You need to be ready, confident, and competent. Nothing less will do.

We old SWOs tend to be cynical, blunt, and sometimes stuck in a distant generational gap, but there is a lot of truth in what we say, and our perspective matters because it is your foundation.

A Definition
of Leadership

When I was in high school, I took U.S. Army JROTC* in an effort to be more competitive for a NROTC scholarship or to try to get into the Naval Academy. We didn't have Naval JROTC, so I was stuck wearing army greens and marching around in the hot Miami sun in the parking lot of the high school. However, our two instructors were fantastic. Both were retired special forces guys who served together on teams over multiple deployments to Vietnam. Now, in retrospect, I realize that I didn't fully appreciate how good they were at teaching and motivating. Duh, that is the mission of special forces—go figure.

One of the things I remember the most (aside from the orienteering courses—I can still work my way through grid coordinates) was the definition of leadership from the army field manual, FM 22-100 (DEC 1958). It stated, "Military Leadership. The art of influencing and directing men in such a way as to obtain their

---

*   Junior Reserve Officers' Training Corps—this is for high school students.

willing obedience, confidence, respect, and loyal cooperation in order to accomplish the mission." Simple and direct.

In the Navy Leader Development Framework (3.0), it describes the leaders that are sought out for the Navy:

> "Navy leaders inspire us to relentlessly chase 'best ever' performance. They study, innovate, experiment, practice, sustain, seize every moment, expend every effort—all to outfox our competition. They connect, communicate, challenge, train, and recover with us. Our Navy leaders are humble; they are open to our meaningful feedback. They are ready to learn and make all of us better. When they win, they are grateful and spent from their effort. Navy leaders form our teams into a community, with a deeply shared commitment, dedicated to the pursuit of victory."

This vision really is just a wordy version of the Army definition from 1958, with an apparent nod to President Theodore Roosevelt. The "so what" is that what makes a good leader really doesn't change.

Personally, I am partial to the Army definition of 1958, but that is me and my leadership style. I offer it to you to consider. After almost thirty-seven years of leading and being led, I thought I could offer you something a little more, something introspective on my part. Good leaders realize that leadership is a bit more nuanced than just a definition.

I'd like you to consider the term that is used in the Army definition: *art*. Today, we are so quick to lean heavily on technology and science to solve warfighting problems and challenges—these technology fixes cannot be applied to leadership. The art of leadership is knowing how and when to use a certain tool of leadership at the right time and place. Technology is just the tool—the art is the application.

As with the art of leadership, there is a parallel effort in the *art* of war. Neither leadership nor war is a mathematical equation; it is a human endeavor that is completely driven by the whims of the human condition. Those conditions are completely driven by the environment and the influences on those humans. What motivates people is as varied as the spectrum of colors, both visible and invisible; likewise are the reasons we go to war. Understanding how to harness motivations—what drives people—and use that to influence them to achieve a common goal is the art.

The Artist's Toolbox

Your leadership style is unique; it is coded in your DNA, and it is your fingerprint that you will leave everywhere you go. Your impact as a leader will either end up looking like a Seurat* masterpiece or a crime scene. It is completely up to you.

We develop our leadership style over years—it is evolutionary. In truth, I believe the best leaders are born, not made. However, people can learn to be good leaders given the right influences, experiences, and learning moments. I look back on both my cadetship and career and recognize the impact (both positive and negative) that leaders had on me and my leadership style. You may be born with the gift of being a natural leader, but the influences of both your leaders and followers will shape the style and application of your leadership.

I am also a firm believer in scar tissue. Scar tissue is tough and uncomfortable; it is a reminder of past wounds—scars may fade, but they don't go away. Sometimes the most lasting

---

* Seurat was an artist who was a pointillist—he used dots, thousands of them, to paint his pictures.

memories and lessons learned are from traumatic experiences that impact the way we think and approach future events. The key is to use all these experiences to build better approaches. In other words, sometimes bad leaders make the best examples because we remember how they affected us and those around us. We become sensitive to those methods, and we color our approach to avoid repeating them. We work very hard not to become them. Conversely, we enjoy good leaders so much that we take their leadership for granted and forget to take notes. So, it is important to remember both styles of leadership and what they did that was effective and not so effective.

There are lots of leaders we want to emulate. Leaders who struck us as larger than life and had a way about them that made you want to follow them anywhere. We all have those individuals in our lives, and we might be lucky enough to have more than one. While you cannot become those people, you can adopt and adapt some of their elements. These are the things we put in our toolbox.

We take these things—our DNA, our experiences, and our lessons—and put them in the leadership toolbox. Again, as the artist, it is up to you to choose and apply the right tool at the right time. That is the challenge and the risk. By being the leader (or the artist to carry the metaphor), your application of your art makes you simultaneously powerful and vulnerable. It takes courage to be a leader.

First and Foremost

As a leader, your job is to facilitate the personal and professional success of your subordinates. You set the environment for them. Their success will be yours.

Organizational success is founded on the people who work for you and with you. You must create an environment for your people to succeed in order for them to reach their full potential.

When new Sailors report to the command, they have to meet with many people upon check-in. The last three people they are supposed to meet with are the Command Master Chief (the senior enlisted person and advisor to the Executive and Commanding Officers), the Executive Officer, and the Commanding Officer. I always had the new check-ins fill out a questionnaire about their educational and professional past, their family life and situation, their hobbies, the last book they read, their personal and professional goals, and why they joined the Navy. I will normally have that to review prior to my check-in with them. The questionnaire will highlight for me a number of things:

- The Sailor's experience
- The Sailor's motivations and interests
- The status of the Sailor's homelife
- A possible common interest to make a personal connection

I also ask that they read my published command mission, vision, and philosophy prior to the check-in. I always ask if they read and understand the mission, vision, and philosophy statements; if they can abide by what I am asking them to; and if they have any questions or concerns about them. My mission, vision, and philosophy statements are clear, concise, and unambiguous. I have to live up to my own standard, and I always express to the Sailors that I expect them to live up to it as well. With that as a baseline, we have a discussion.

My pledge to the Sailor is that I will facilitate their personal and professional success, but it is up to the Sailor to define what that looks like to them and to use the tools I provide to get there. If they are missing a tool, it is their responsibility to ask. No one joins the Navy to fail. I don't think any Sailor who raised their right hand thought to themselves, *I am going to set out to make a train wreck of my life while I am here in the Navy.* When things go sideways and a good Sailor gets off track, engaged and observant leadership can usually detect the wheels becoming wobbly and can right the train.

Along these lines is something else that can easily be mistaken for micromanagement or intrusive leadership (which I think is fine): Learn and become familiar with the jobs of your subordinates; that will allow you to be an effective advocate for them. If you don't take the time to learn what your Sailors do, you will never understand the depth and breadth of their expertise, their knowledge and experience, or their enthusiasm for their job and the satisfaction that goes along with it. This applies both in the service and out of the service—good leaders in all walks of life should have an appreciation of the work that is being done by their subordinates. That appreciation builds trust and a sense of team spirit.

As a Division Officer, you probably won't have a mission, vision, or philosophy statement;* it is not expected of you, but you should welcome your new Sailor, get to know them, and make sure that they are acclimating to the command. Make sure you clearly express your expectations of your Sailor, and what they can expect from you. You should make sure your Division Officer's Notebook is up-to-date. Each Sailor in your division should have a section. In it, there should be a bio sheet of some kind, and it should look a lot like the CO's intake interview above but usually has a lot more detail. Some Divos let their Chiefs manage the Divo Notebook. I did not. I let my CPOs comanage the notebook with me. Most times, you will conduct counseling and/or mentoring together anyway, so keeping it in your possession is just fine from my perspective.

---

* Of course, that isn't to say you can't have an MVP. If you do choose to develop one for yourself and your division, make sure it is aligned with your commanding officer's MVP.

5

"Ensigns Should Be Seen and Not Heard"

Eyes and ears open, mouth shut.

When I checked aboard my first ship in December 1993, I showed up—based on the advice of the Fleet Lieutenant* instructors at Surface Warfare Officer School, Division Officer Course (SWOSDOC)—on Friday at lunchtime. When I arrived at the ship, there was a group of carolers on the quarterdeck serenading the watch standers. The carolers were a bunch of Disney characters. This was my first impression of the ship. It seemed pretty welcoming. As the Mouseketeers left the quarterdeck, I made my way up the accommodation ladder ("acomm" ladder), put my sea bag down, and presented myself to the Officer of the Deck (OOD). He signed my orders and gave me directions to get to the wardroom where the Command Duty Officer (CDO) was eating lunch, and he told me, "Most of the

---

* Fleet Lieutenants were those Lieutenants who had been successful out in the fleet and came back to instruct at the school. These Lieutenants were experienced, knowledgeable, and salty.

ship is already on liberty. The CDO will tell you where to drop your stuff." I hoisted my sea bag onto my shoulder and headed up to the wardroom.

When I entered the wardroom, I placed my sea bag on the deck in the lounge and went into the dining room. I then presented myself to the CDO, who was a Lieutenant Junior Grade (LTjg). "Good morning, sir. I am Ensign Nilsson, and I am reporting for duty. May I join you for lunch?"

He didn't even look up from his plate before growling at me. "Ensigns should be seen and not heard. Sit down." He then finished his lunch and left. Not nearly as welcoming as the quarterdeck. I thought to myself, *Well, that was rude!* That afternoon, the only thoughts I was left with were: *What do I do? What is expected of me? And where the hell do I drop my stuff?*

My father gave me great advice as I headed off for that first ship: "Keep your eyes and ears open, and keep your mouth shut." In retrospect, I think it was kind of the same advice and direction I received from the LTjg, but Dad was nicer about it, and it was not veiled in an unwelcoming SWO growl. So, what are the expectations of a newly reported Ensign? COs, XOs, and department heads all have different expectations, and you have to be aware of them. But as a former Commanding Officer, here are mine:

Divo Expectations:

- Be honest, but tactful.
- Be aggressive, but humble.
- Learn your job, and do it.

- Listen to your CPOs.
- Get qualified quickly, but thoroughly.
- Be professionally curious.
- Have fun.

All pretty simple but nuanced at the same time. They are all linked. They all also tie into the concept of eyes and ears open, mouth shut. They all involve active learning and developing as a junior officer.

6

Right the Ship

I was exceptionally driven—I wanted to qualify as a Surface Warfare Officer and laterally transfer. I cranked out my Personal Qualification Standards (PQS) in record time, qualified in all my watch stations, and then some; I became the best Divo I thought I could be. And I could drive the hell out of the ship. In fact, I loved standing watch and driving the ship. Within six months, I finished all my SWO requirements with the exception of Officer of the Deck, Underway, and I was just waiting on my oral examination. But, writ large, I did not follow my dad's advice very well, nor did I heed the advice of the LTjg—to my own detriment. I was cocky, opinionated, and stubborn. My guys loved me and were fiercely loyal, but I was not welcome in the wardroom among my peers. I had a couple of friends, but by and large, I was dismissed as brash and impetuous. It turned out to be a very lonely two and a half years—all self-inflicted.

With hindsight and distance, I realized that I really had some great mentors on that ship. The Warrant Officers and Limited Duty Officers (LDO) took me under their wings, as did the Chief

Petty Officers' (CPO) mess and my second department head. I was fortunate that the first CO and XO I worked for liked me and saw the potential in me that didn't really come alive until my second tour, but the second CO and XO did not like me at all. The fact that I didn't like them either did not play into my favor—again, it was more self-inflicted than anything else.

As an Ensign right out of college, just know that when you get to the fleet, everyone knows more than you do. Even if they don't, they do. Just accept that. The Warrants and LDOs are typically experts in their fields and have seen just about everything the Navy could throw at them. They will be quick to tell you how messed up you are, but they will work extra hard to train you. Never turn down the opportunity to receive mentorship from these men and women. Through all my command tours, I learned from those men and women every day.

The Chiefs are the technical experts and can run your division better than you can. Listen and learn. Part of their job is to make you successful. My opinion about the Chiefs' mess over the years is like a sine wave—it is a constant up and down. In the aggregate, though, I've had more good Chiefs than bad Chiefs, and 90 percent of the Master Chiefs I have worked with are rock stars.

Your department heads will crush you with tasking, eat you alive in front of your division, then turn around and mentor you, comfort you, and teach you how to be effective. They want you to work them out of a job. My First Lieutenant, whom I mentioned earlier, was, at first, a scary woman. She was one of the first female officers to be selected and assigned to an afloat combatant; she had been a naval aviator, served on oilers, and came to make her mark on our ship. And leave a mark she did.

We did not get along at first. When turning over with her predecessor, the report she got on me was "shitbag." Her perspective on me was set, and it was not good. But by this point, I was already almost two years into my tour, and the reality was that I knew my business really well. I had survived my tour in engineering as the E-Divo and was now in the deck department as the First and Second Division Officer (we were short an officer in the department). I was responsible for all the topside gear, the flight deck, the well deck, and all the Marine spaces. After a few minor brush-ups over little things, we ended up in a very heated argument, which ended with her threatening to get me assigned to a radar posting in Adak, Alaska. I replied that that would be a massive improvement over my current situation. Now, what I should have done was keep my mouth shut and cool down a bit. Instead, I left the ship early and without permission. She had every right to get me thrown off the ship and posted to Alaska.

Boat Officer, 1994, off Camp Pendleton, California

To her credit, this exchange bothered her. She went to my CPOs and my E-6s to see what their opinions of me were. As I said before, my Sailors were exceptionally loyal, and this was evident to her. She called me Saturday morning and asked if I had Rollerblades (this was the '90s). I said no, and she replied, "No matter, get your running shoes on. I will be by to pick you up in fifteen minutes." She hung up before I could say anything. My first thought was, *I am really hungover.* Second thought: *How the hell does she even know where I live?*

We went up to Lake Murray, where there is a four-mile asphalt trail around the lake. She skated and I ran. It sucked, but we talked the whole way and worked things out. She fired questions at me on how I managed things, how I led my Sailors, and what my processes were. I fired back with answers. We wrapped up the afternoon at Shakespeare's Pub over a couple pints of Guinness. I guess you could say we came to an understanding at that point. And for me, some things began to come out of the fog.

Back on the ship the next week, I showed her everything we did from scheduling to managing the budget. She was impressed and asked why her predecessor didn't know anything about this. I replied, "Because he didn't ask." It was at that moment that a lot became clear. I realized I had done a horrible job of communicating up my chain of command. Not only did I not do myself any favors, but my lack of communication also had the same bad effect on the reputation of the department and my Sailors. My first real lesson learned in communication. From this moment on, though, we went from being dirtbags to overnight rock stars. The First Lieutenant and I established a solid relationship. She was my first true department head mentor, and she set me on a path to love what we do as Surface Warfare Officers.

To a great degree, this was one of the lowest points during my first tour. I really didn't like the environment I was in, and I felt underappreciated and misunderstood. In reality, I was unbalanced and struggling to fit in. What I expected out of my leadership (with the exception of the First Lieutenant) by that point fell way short. And what I expected of myself fell way short. My First Lieutenant, who was struggling with her own challenges of being a pioneer female officer on a combatant, recognized my potential and mentored me. She saw that I had the tools and the artistry to go along with them, but I needed to be directed, advised, and encouraged. She righted my ship. These are the leaders we seek and those we wish to emulate.

7

Credibility

During my time as E-Divo, I had a very diverse division filled with multiple rates. In my division, I had the electrician's mates (EMs), the interior communications men (ICs), and the journalist specialist (JO—now called mass communications specialists (MCs)). Before I went to my first ship, I attended the Diesel Engineering Officer of the Watch School in Newport, Rhode Island. It was really a fantastic school with exceptionally patient and engaged instructors—all enlisted Sailors. The only portion of the course I completely bombed was the electrical engineering section. Naturally, I was assigned to the role of E-Divo on my first ship.

Within a few months of reporting, we had a casualty to the degaussing system on the ship. This system passes (or impresses) a current through the hull of the ship that basically neutralizes the natural magnetic field (or, as we call it, the magnetic signature) of the ship to make it less vulnerable to magnetically-influenced mines. My Sailors determined that the fault was a circuit card that failed and needed replacing. Because we could not fix it quickly (we did not have the part on hand), we had to transmit a casualty report (CASREP) that notified our operational commanders that this particular system was broken and requested expedited shipping of the part. As the E-Divo, it was my responsibility to draft the CASREP and route it up through the chain of command to the CO for release—this was my first time doing so.

The first stop in the chain after I drafted it was the Chief Engineer, Cheng, who had no changes (or as we call them, chops), which was rare because, I later found out, he always had changes. Next, it went to the Supply Officer (Suppo) for his review of the parts-ordering information—no chops there. Next, I took it to the Operations Officer (Ops) to make sure all the addresses were correct and it was formatted correctly. All good there, too. The Executive Officer took his chops on it next, and he always had something to add. So then it was back to the computer (at that point in the early 1990s it was a glorified typewriter, Word 5.0 that saved to five-inch floppy discs) to make the changes, then back to the XO for his final chops and approval to route to the CO. Last stop—the CO.

When I got to the CO's cabin, it was two hours into this routing process—lots of standing in lines, hunting down individuals, and making corrections. As I nervously waited in line outside the CO's cabin, I could hear the other Divos routing their messages, and they didn't seem to have any issues. I relaxed a little bit. This was my first CO on the ship; he was awesome, patient, and understanding. When it was my turn, I entered his cabin and handed him the CASREP. He read it and then started asking me questions about the system and what was wrong with it. Wait, what? He didn't ask any of the other guys any questions! Why me? And these were questions I was not prepared to answer! Where was the card located, how did I know it was the faulty part, what was the overall impact on the other coils, how long would it take to get the part, and others? I had no answers other than, "I don't know, but I will find out." He looked at me over his reading glasses and said, "Erik, I am really disappointed in you. I expected more. Please find out the answers to my questions, and then I'll release your CASREP. You are dismissed." I was utterly devastated. The worst thing I could ever hear from this man: *I am disappointed in you.* So why did he rake me over the coals and send me away? Credibility. I had zero credibility on the ship at that point. The other officers had been on the ship for months, if not years, longer than I had, and they had all the credibility they needed.

I spent the next two hours with my Sailors pouring through the technical manuals (TECHMAN) and reading the line diagrams, going to the site of the casualty, having them show me how to test the card myself, and having my Sailors show me the process on how to run a bit test on the system. Armed with that knowledge, the TECHMANs under my arm, and my leading EM in tow, I went back up to the CO's cabin for another run at it.

I laid out the line diagrams and explained how we arrived at the faulty card, how we tested the card in the shop, and how we ran the bit tests on the rest of the coils to make sure this was not a cascading casualty that would affect other parts of the system. All the while, my EM1 was standing behind me, nodding at the CO. When I was done explaining the process, the troubleshooting procedures we used, and how it was actually a series of resistors and microswitches that went bad on the card, but we still had to order the whole card, he put his hands on his hips and smiled. He said, "This is what I expect of you every time you come into my cabin." This was a major step in building my professional credibility with the captain.

You have to build and rebuild credibility with each and every command you go to. Your credibility is inextricably linked to your reputation, and rest assured that it will precede you. One of my bosses used to say, "Credibility is the coin of the realm." You don't need to become a technical expert on what your Sailors are trained to do, but you do need to have a good understanding of what they do. In building that understanding, you become both a better advocate for your Sailors and a trusted and respected member of the wardroom. You will be credible.

Liberty and Accountability

As I look back over my career, especially those times during liberty ports on my first cruise, I am surprised I made it as far as I did and am still alive. I don't necessarily look back with rose-colored glasses and think, *Oh, those were the good ol' days.* I am not that naïve, but those days do make for some amazing stories.

When we pulled into Phuket, Thailand, in the summer of 1994, there was a laundry list of things "Thou Shalt Not" do. Sailors shall not: engage in Muay Thai (or what we have come to recognize as kickboxing/MMA), bungee jump, paraglide, ride on local conveyances such as motor scooters, drink to excess, visit the houses of ill repute, venture into the off-limits areas, and others. There was a brief on the ship's TV channel the night before we pulled in, but I was on watch at the time. But much like the honor code at VMI, ignorance was no excuse. I was supposed to have a few days of liberty (time off), but because I had work to do on the ship, I couldn't leave with the first few boats or "liberty launches," so I was a few hours behind everyone else. And while today we have to depart and return with our liberty buddies, back then it was only strongly suggested that you have a liberty buddy, but you could head off on your own. The only stipulation was that you show up for your duty day, or final liberty expiration.

We were anchored just off the island, so we had to take a boat into the fleet landing and then take a bus to the town. I remember riding the bus from fleet landing to the drop-off point in the town of Phuket. I sat next to the marine expeditionary unit (MEU) chaplain. He was a Catholic priest, a Lieutenant Colonel, and about as Irish as they get. He offered me a taste from his flask and asked me what my plans were for the port visit. I really had none. His advice: always go out with a plan. I should have had a plan.

The JOs rented a small bungalow close to the beach, and I went there first to drop off my stuff. After that, I headed out to see if I could find my buddies. The only thing that I had to do that evening was show up at a Hail and Farewell (welcoming the new officers and saying goodbye to the ones departing) for some of the officers at a local restaurant—but that was hours away.

Thailand is hot, and it is really easy to get thirsty while walking around. There was a ton to see and experience, and I wanted to take it all in. My first stop was an exhibition Muay Thai fighting ring. You could watch and place bets on the fighters and get cold Singha beers. I thought, *What a great place to get a beer!* I sat down near the ring and promptly pulled on my first beer. Cold, wet, and refreshing. As I sat and enjoyed my beer, a couple of Marines joined me at my table, and a couple of local expats were next to us. We all started chatting about the boxers, their relative speed, technique, and flair. Now, having taken boxing and wrestling at VMI, I could understand the tactics used by the fighters in the ring and could appreciate the physicality of the spectacle. There is a beauty to Muay Thai fighting as well as a brutality that is unmatched. It really was thrilling. So thrilling that, three beers later, I wanted to give it a try and was enthusiastically encouraged by my new best friends.

I sauntered up to the guy who seemed to be in charge and asked if anyone could try. Why yes, I could give it a try. The establishment often allowed spectators to pay to get in the ring for a few rounds to see how long they could last with a couple of fighters. My new best friends ponied up the banka bucks with gusto. They had a lot of faith in me and showed their faith by cheering me on loudly. Their cheers drew a crowd from folks outside on the street. To be clear, though, this was an open-air ring under a roof, so the outside was just off the curb. Everyone could see.

I got into the ring and took off my shirt and shoes, did a few stretches, shadowboxed a bit, and got a little coaching from some local instructor and the staff sergeant who was one of my new buddies. I was ready. The bell rang, and out bounced this little Thai fighter. Money was changing hands as bets flew around the ring. I was a little bigger than this guy, but I was untested, and the bets were predominantly against me—go figure. The fighter and I danced around a little, jabs and elbows, a few tentative kicks from the Thai, and I saw an opening. A memory flashed in my mind of the VMI boxing coach yelling from the side of the ring in the VMI boxing room, "He's open, finish it!" I let loose with a right hook and laid the guy out. The crowd went nuts. Well, this was pretty easy! I was sweating again from the bit of physical exertion and excitement, and I needed another beer in between rounds.

The second fight was a bit longer; the Thai fighter was a little better, but oddly, I won again with a combination of boxing moves and some wrestling that was really just frantic grappling. The crowd had grown even more with lots of spectators. I was getting cheered very loudly now, and my confidence was way up—for a second. Now, I know I am pretty good in a fight, but even through the growing fog of the beer, I started to think this was too easy. Money was exchanging hands again around the ring, the crowd was electric and booming, and odds were tilting in my favor among the less-informed bettors. I took some water instead of beer and looked at my next opponent across the ring. Something was off. He looked calm, cool, and determined—not that the other two were not, but I am pretty sure he knew something that I didn't.

When the bell rang to start the third fight, I was suddenly very tired. My opponent was not. He was evenly matched with me size-wise and had an amazing Jean-Claude Van Damme physique. I had a two-months-of-underway-and-hot-cinnamon-sticky-buns-on-the-mid-watch physique. The guy came at me like a spider monkey on a speeding freight train. I watched in awe and amazement as his fists and feet flew in a blur of movement around my head. It was so cool to watch this guy go; he was so good. I am not sure I even had the chance to get my hands up in a defensive posture. I felt the first foot land on my right ear, and then it was over. I heard later that he roundhoused my left ear.

A bit later, I woke up in a chair with a cold beer next to me, a stack of baht (Thai currency) that I "earned" on the first two fights, and a slight headache. My new best friends headed off to look for other entertainment, and I decided to head to the beach to rest my head.

There is lots to do and see on the beach in Thailand. Phuket is a resort area with lots of beach activities, and they all looked fun. With my newfound wealth, I decided to try out a few things I had never had the opportunity to do. First: bungee jump. What could go wrong? I mean, when you get latched into a harness, clipped into the great big rubber band, and hoisted up on a crane that probably came in with the Marines during the Vietnam era, there has to be some science and safety protocols that make this all good. I didn't look, and I didn't really care. Oh, did I mention that they were offering shooters on the beach? The bungee jump—or actually bungee drop because all they do is hoist you up to the ball of the crane hook and push a button that releases the pelican hook attached to the harness—is pretty thrilling, and it is done over the water. Safe, right? Well, good for everyone else, it was over the water, because when the bungee cord reached its farthest reach, I lost the contents of my stomach. Which, frankly, was the cleanest way to hurl: right into the water. And because of the swing of the bungee cord, I was lowered into the water about ten feet from where I had just chummed.

Walking back to the beach, I saw a speedboat go by with a parasail coming off its back. That looked really cool. I'd seen it done in Miami, but it always cost too much to try it out. I still had baht to blow! I got back to the beach and looked at my watch—plenty of time to make the Hail and Farewell. And I was more or less sober. I walked down the beach to the landing of the parasail boats, and one was unoccupied, save the driver and his really pretty assistant. I was all in. I handed over the cash and away we went. No surprise, they had a cooler of Singha—cold and refreshing! I took a long pull on the beer, and the gal helped me get into the harness for the parasail, which looked really similar to the one from the bungee jump. At this point, the wind kicked up a little, and the driver said we would have to wait a few minutes for the wind to calm down—safety first. Yeah, whatever, just enough time to have another beer. We waited a bit and I chatted up the girl. Super nice. Anyway, we got our chance, we picked up speed, the sail billowed behind me, and up I went. As cool as it looked, the experience delivered. It was a great view and really fun. I did not throw up on this ride. After I was recovered and we made our way back to the beach, I looked at my watch and realized I did not account for going back to the hotel and changing in order to get to the Hail and Farewell on time. I was now late. My new friend from the boat said, "I have scooter and can take you—for fee."

"For free?" I asked.

"No," she said. "For *fee*." Oh. Here you go, ma'am! And away we went! I also had to pay for the beers on the boat. Quick lesson: nothing is free in Thailand.

I hopped on the back of the scooter and held on for dear life. I am not sure how many baht busses* and trucks we narrowly missed, nor could I recount how we made it to the Hail and Farewell without a scratch. But we arrived just on time. The event was held at a restaurant that, like most, was open-air in the front, and that is where our wardroom was gathered. Not everyone was there yet, but most were there. So, when I hopped off the scooter and ambled into the restaurant, I realized that

---

* The "baht bus" is Sailor slang for the open-air scooter taxis that would take you anywhere for only a few baht, the Thai currency.

everyone who was on the veranda was staring at me. I wasn't underdressed, nor was I late, so I wondered why.

Immediately I was surrounded by the other JOs and pummeled with questions: Were you really parasailing? Did you really do a bungee jump? Did we really see you in the Thai boxing ring? Did you know that all of that is forbidden? Uh, yes, yes, yes, and what? One of the LTjgs pulled me aside and said that the XO was looking for me and that he was not happy. And then he called me an idiot. I went to find the XO.

Our XO at the time actually liked me. He was a prince of a guy—fair, intelligent, deliberate, even-tempered, and had a great sense of humor. I did not appreciate at the time that I worked for him just how good he was. Fortunately, we ran into each other years later, and I expressed my gratitude for his great example. Sadly, he passed away a few years ago from cancer—a great officer taken from us too soon. However, at this point, he was mad at me. I mean, really mad. I walked straight up to him and said, "XO, I am pretty sure I screwed up, sir."

His eyes bored through mine to the back of my skull as he calmly said, "Of course you did." He then said, "As soon as we are done here, you will report directly back to the ship." My reply: "Yes, sir."

Well, that was sobering. When the event was over, I hopped in a taxi, swung by the bungalow to grab my stuff, and went straight to the fleet landing. I didn't really talk to anyone at the Hail and Farewell. All I could think of was, "Of course you did." Did he see me as that much of a screwup? Did he think I was insubordinate? Did he think I was just useless? All this and more swirled around in my head and made me sick to my stomach. Was I going to go to Captain's Mast?

When I got back to the ship, I found that I had beat the XO back and went to shower and get in my uniform. Once cleaned up, I reported straight to the XO's stateroom. It was now 21:00, and he still hadn't returned. I stood there in the dark until 01:00, when he came back. He looked at me and said, "I will see you at 09:00."

The next morning, I reported as directed. I don't think I'd felt this way since answering my first special with the commandant at VMI, but I didn't have my Dyke* to back me up. I was on my own. I thought to myself, *Own all of it. You have no one to blame but yourself. Take the ass-chewing and drive on.* I knocked on the door and heard, "Enter." I reported as directed and remained at attention. He looked up at me over his reading glasses and said, "Do you realize the position you've put your CO in?" Not the question I was anticipating. I started to say, "I guess—" and he cut me off. "Nope, I want you to think about this one before answering." I hadn't really thought about the CO's position, except for the possibility of nonjudicial punishment (NJP), or what is commonly referred to as Captain's Mast.

For the most part, a junior Sailor can survive NJP and motor on with his or her career. Usually, it is recoverable and

---

* Special Reports and Dykes at VMI. At VMI, a Special is a Special Report—a written order to report to the commandant for an infraction of the rules. It is a lot like nonjudicial punishment in the military, but the punishment at VMI is marching penalty tours, being awarded demerits, and being remanded to the VMI post or barracks for a period of time. The Dyke system at VMI is similar to a big brother-little brother system in the Greek system. A senior will pick a freshman (also known as a Rat at VMI) to be his or her Dyke and will mentor that Rat for the first year, show him or her the ropes, and guide that Rat through the maze of VMI. It is a special relationship that in some cases last a lifetime.

more like a speed bump than a career-ender, depending on the severity of the infraction. For officers, NJP is pretty much a career-ender. I put the CO in the position of having to decide whether to end my career or not. I had violated fleet policies multiple times within a twelve-hour period. He had to do something. On the other hand, the CO really liked me—that I knew. I was a hard worker, thoughtful, loyal to my Sailors, a solid shiphandler, and a motivated officer. This put him in a horrible position. I conveyed all this to the XO. I also followed up with an acknowledgment of my transgressions, a willingness to accept any and all punishment, that I was very sorry, and that the decisions were mine alone and I had no one else to blame but myself. That was where he stopped me again. He said, "Erik, the CO and I have discussed this at length, and we both knew that you would take full accountability for your actions. We also determined that you do need to be punished. The CO will see us in his cabin in ten minutes."

My stomach fell. I had a pretty good idea of what was coming my way. To a certain extent, VMI trains you to face the music. I had my share of answering specials in the commandant's office, and for the most part, you knew the punishment that you were going to receive when you walked into the office. This was the same, but really different. This really mattered. I didn't have a "correct, but wish to explain" option here. There is one thing I will also highlight here. It was really easy for me to fall on my sword and completely admit to the transgressions—I had no one else I was responsible for, and frankly, if I had to leave the service, I could go home and start over relatively easily. If I had a wife, maybe some college debt, or other big responsibilities hanging over my head, I might not have been as quick to admit everything. That doesn't mean I wouldn't have, but I certainly may have been more deliberate. This is where your ethics come into play.

I've heard the statement, "Ethics is what you do when no one is looking." The Oxford Dictionary defines ethics as "moral principles that govern a person's behavior or the conduct of an activity." The honor code at VMI states that a Cadet "will not lie, cheat, or steal, nor tolerate those who do." That code, which is spliced into your DNA at VMI, can and will guide your ethical choices. Do the right thing. Ideally, I should have avoided getting into this situation from the start.

The Captain restricted me to the ship for the rest of the port visit (what we now call Liberty Risk) except for my duty-day responsibility on shore patrol. I did my shift and reported right back to the ship (whereas the other guys could stay out in town). I had to meet with my department head, XO, and CO before the next port visit to reassess my viability to even go on liberty, and I was assigned to the first day of duty for the remainder of the deployment, no matter what section had the watch. I was also required to have a liberty buddy.

I mentioned earlier about credibility and reputation. You are continually building it with every day, every tour, and every decision. My credibility and reputation took a hit that day. Toward the end of deployment, the XO, who had only a few weeks left on the ship, had me in his cabin, and we talked about a CASREP I was routing at the time. I maintained a mostly clean liberty slate for the rest of my deployment. He asked me if I remembered our conversation at the restaurant in Phuket, where he said, "Of course you did." I told him I did, and that it had stung. He said that he knew I was going to get into some kind of trouble at some point on deployment because I had a rebellious streak a mile wide and a natural inclination to be dismissive of authority and headstrong. And a continuous, self-driven disposition to prove something to everyone. He said that I had enormous potential as a leader and as a naval officer, and if I didn't learn how to harness all that energy for good, I was going to fail spectacularly. He dismissed me, saying, "Okay, you can go and finish routing that CASREP now." As I turned and headed out of his cabin, he said, "Hey Erik, you know, if you do figure out how to harness all that, there is no limit to how far you can go or how much you can achieve. People will follow you anywhere. Be careful where you lead them."

Building Relationships

When I detached from my first ship, I had to take a couple of courses at schools en route to my next ship. I was assigned as the navigator, so I had to attend Senior Quartermaster Refresher, then on to Celestial Navigation. But first, I was temporarily assigned—or, as we call it, "stashed"—to the Immediate Superior in Command (ISIC) on the amphibious squadron (PHIBRON) staff for a couple of weeks before my schools started. When I arrived, I reported in, and almost immediately I had a meeting with the Commodore. He said, "I have some tasking for you. What is your plan?" I told him that I had to get some medical things taken care of, some admin fixed, and a pay issue resolved. I told him I needed about an entire work week (about five days) to get everything done. He looked at me, perplexed. See, all that was supposed to be taken care of by the ship when I detached—and it wasn't for a lack of effort on my part. I detached in such a hurry that I was more or less handed my detaching package and my award on the quarterdeck and sent off. The ship deployed later that morning. Normally, you would have a few weeks to get all the paperwork together, get all the medical screenings accomplished, and be "farewelled" at a Hail and Farewell party. None of that happened—and sometimes, that just happens.

The Commodore asked to see my detaching package, and I handed it over. First, he looked at the award, then at me, then at the award again. He said, "Well, this is wrong."

I said, "Yes, sir."

My name had been spelled wrong. He then looked at the rest of the paperwork. I had detailed a list of things I needed to get done, which was on top of the stack of papers. He looked at it, scratched his head, and said, "Okay, knock all this out. But as I mentioned, I have a job for you." He then told me about the list of CASREPs that the ship had when it left. Mostly, it was for parts that should have been onboard before they left. But they didn't make it onboard because they didn't have the correct priority assigned to them. He said, "Figure out what you can do to get them the parts by the time they get to Hawaii, and we will help you with getting your stuff squared away."

I took the stack of CASREPs from him along with my detaching package and said, "Yes sir, not a problem."

I made friends with anyone who could help me, like the various shop Chiefs at SIMA (Ship's Intermediate Maintenance Availability—now called RMCs (Regional Maintenance Centers)). One time I traded a pound of "wardroom coffee" and our broken shore power breaker for a new shore power breaker. I also made friends with the special boat team bubbas, who let me raid their boats that were being decommissioned for parts and bling and their supply boxes for cleaning gear to round out our deployment stash. The point being: make friends with everyone, and never burn bridges.

Over the course of my first tour, I made friends with the fleet supply ladies. A lot of things get done with a phone call or email, but good old face-to-face interaction is the best. If you need parts expedited, the fleet supply professionals are the ones to make friends with. Whenever we needed parts quickly, my Chief and I would head downtown to the fleet supply offices and bring sweets to the expediters—back then, a group of super nice ladies. Being in Engineering during my first tour, I spent a lot of time in that building. Now, with the stack of CASREPs the Commodore handed me, I headed over to the fleet supply office. I drove over with a quick stop at the store along the way. When I got to the floor where the fleet supply ladies had their desks, I issued hugs and boxes of Whitman's chocolates. Ostensibly, I was there to say goodbye and to say thanks—they'd saved my bacon more than once. Of course, along with some storytelling, I told them about the lamentable condition of the CASREPs and my "impossible" tasking. One of the ladies, the parts expediter, said, "If only you had the stamp that I have in my bottom left drawer, and your worries would be over . . ." Then she said (and I am not making this up) with a wink, "Let's go to lunch, ladies!"

The parts successfully met the ship in Hawaii. And of course, I went home at lunch because there was surfing to be done. When I got back to the PHIBRON offices the next day, I dropped off the copies of the top pages of the CASREPs with the EXPEDITED stamp on top to the N4 (the supply officer). He asked, "Hey, who are you, and how did you do this?"

I replied, "I am LTjg Nilsson and I am stashed here. And I know people." Always protect your sources.

I was only at PHIBRON for two weeks. I got all my stuff

fixed and taken care of the first week, so for the second week I did whatever the staff wanted me to do—mostly write messages and review things. When I checked out with the Commodore, he remarked what a help I'd been over the past two weeks. He also asked about the CASREPs and how I did them. I said he didn't want to know, and he laughed and said I was probably right. But what he said last stuck with me. He went on to say how disappointed he was with my previous ship's CO and the state in which they left me, saying, "This is not what we do to our people, not how we take care of them." He said he didn't know I was coming over to be stashed until the morning I showed up. It was simply poor form all around. He then said, "I don't know what your reputation was on the ship, but in the short time you've been here, you have established yourself as a hardworking and dependable officer, and from what I've seen, a very resourceful one. I know your next CO, and I am going to let him know what a good man he is getting onboard. Best of luck, and don't make a liar out of me."

Relationships are important. I relearned a lesson I had been taught through the Rat Line at VMI—no one makes it through alone. There are hundreds of people outside of an operational command who help make a ship or unit successful. Many times, we get frustrated with these people because of a process they must follow or a rule they must adhere to—but those processes and rules are there to ensure equitable load-sharing for all the ships and units. But if you form good relationships with these people, they will work just a little harder for you and might even skip a few steps in the process to help you out. A smile, a brief office visit, and a kind word go a long way toward building those relationships. And chocolates—chocolates go a long way.

10

Gator

The Navy is a large organization that expects you to perform from day one. It is tough and challenging, but sometimes the Navy, mostly inadvertently, throws you a bone. Sometimes we just get the coolest opportunities. When I transferred to my second ship, the USS CURTS (FFG 38)—"The .38 Special"—I got to meet it in Singapore. I had been to Singapore once before and loved it. It is still my favorite port. When I arrived, it was around midnight, and there was no one at the airport to meet me, so I headed to the taxi queue. At the head of the taxi queue that night was "Bob." I don't know his real name, but as he loaded my bags into the taxi's trunk, he told me to call him "Bob." Bob recognized that I was not sure where to go, and my sea bags were a dead giveaway that I was a U.S. Sailor. He suggested a hotel. I had no idea where I was even authorized to go, but he asked my rank and knew what was in my authorized per diem. He took me to The Inn of Seventh Happiness in Old Chinatown—and no, it wasn't *that* type of place. It was, however, one of the coolest hotels I have ever stayed in. He offered to meet me the next morning to take me to Sembawang, where my ship was going to be. I agreed.

I got up early and went for a run through the old streets and back alleys to explore and reset my internal clock (this became a habit over the years while traveling). As the sun came up, the heat kicked in, and soon I was drenched. I got back to the hotel, showered, and put on my uniform. Bob picked me up promptly at 08:00, and we headed over to the port. When we arrived, there was no CURTS. The ship was nowhere in sight. He took me to the offices of COMLOG WESTPAC there in the port, and I was told that my ship would not arrive for five days. Are you kidding me? I had five days in Singapore by myself.

When the ship eventually pulled in, I was on the pier waiting with Bob, who, by the way, became my and the JOs' unofficial driver whenever we were in Singapore. When I made it up to the bridge and met with the commanding officer, I introduced myself and said I intended on being his navigator and the admin officer, and I wanted my own quasi-department—this was a bold move for a newly reporting junior officer. Heck, I'd only been aboard for about thirty minutes. He squinted and looked at me in a bemused way and said, "Sure, just work it out with Ops." Then he noticed Bob and his vehicle on the pier and said, "Ah, I love Singapore. There is my car and driver."

I hesitated for a second and sheepishly said, "Well, sir, that is actually my car and driver." Then there was this awkward silence between us.

He looked at me and said, "Well, okay, good luck with Ops. Welcome aboard."

As it turned out, Ops was not thrilled with my idea. In fact, the minute I introduced myself to him and laid out my intent, he pretty much lost his mind. "Who the hell do you think you are?" he shouted. "What makes you think you can walk in here and dictate to me what you are going to do and who you are going to work for? That isn't how things work around here, Lieutenant JUNIOR GRADE!" As he was yelling at me, I noticed over his shoulder a T-shirt hanging on a hook with a very distinctive design on the pocket. So I asked him, "Is that your T-shirt?"

He said, "Yeah—so what?!"

I then stuck out my hand and reintroduced myself. "Erik Nilsson, Class of 1993, Bravo Company."

He looked at me, looked at the shirt, looked back at me, and sighed. "Of course you are VMI." I became Nav-Admin that afternoon.

You may recall that I said we all have folks whom we want to emulate or be like. Now that I was to be the ship's navigator, I thought about our second navigator on my first ship, Mike. Mike was one of the most talented mariners I have ever known. He is who I most wanted to be like: cool under pressure, could visualize his plan and execute it, was a master navigator, a superior shiphandler, could read the weather like a book, and had an awesome sense of humor. To this day, we are still close friends, and we are both in seafaring professions. Mike was always well prepared. He spent hours on his charts and hours preparing for navigation details. His team was well-oiled, and he trained them so that comms were minimal and succinct; bearing readings were crisp and clear; and transitions between fixes, points of reference, or charts were seamless. His navigation was flawless, his fixes were like asterisks and not loose triangles, we were always on time, and we always knew where we were. I wanted to be like Mike. We called Mike "Gator." Now, "Gator" was fitting for a couple of reasons. First, we were on an amphibious ship which is called a "Gator," so that fit pretty well. And the second and obvious reason is that it is short for navigator. So, again, I wanted to be like Mike. I was now the navigator of a FFG, and I wanted to be called "Gator."

Mr. Vice, Dining Out, in 1997 in Yokosuka, Japan

Now, I felt like I finally had my chance. In Singapore, later that afternoon, I met up with the junior officers, and we all piled into Bob's taxi to head out to town. Over my five days of exploring on my own, I found Molly Malone's Irish Pub on the Boat Quay, so that's where we went. Over a few pints of Guinness, we were all getting to know one another, and I remarked that I wanted to be called "Gator." Quick hint: don't come up with your own nickname. It doesn't work out. Ever. From that moment on, and for a good part of my tour, I was called everything but "Gator." Most I can't print here, but we settled on (at the CO's insistence) "Nav."

In my opinion, being a ship's navigator is one of the coolest jobs you can have—you really do learn the art and science of our naval profession. Your responsibility is massive, and along with it comes the accountability that your peers do not have. You alone are accountable to the CO for getting the ship safely from point A to point B on time and in an efficient manner, as well as setting the ship up for tactical success. I relished the challenges that harbor transits like Surabaya, Indonesia, provided. We had to navigate through a poorly marked channel with a non-English-speaking pilot, up a winding river, through a blinding rainstorm, and underpowered tugs at the pier. Or transits like Lumut, Malaysia, where the ship had previously run aground and this was our first time navigating the transit since that incident (no pucker factor there, right?). Even Hong Kong Harbor—early morning approach before dawn and easily thirty ships, trawlers, and tramp steamers all converging on the same entry point. Yokosuka, Japan—where you have to cross Tokyo Wan at a flank bell to avoid the southbound traffic and quickly enter the harbor. Navigating was fun and challenging, and as hairy as some of the transits were, I enjoyed every one of them.

To a certain extent, I underestimated the amount of work that would go into the admin side of the house. Admin is one of those underrated and unappreciated shops that no one cares about when things go right (which they routinely do), but everyone loses their minds over when things go wrong. In order to have a clear mind for operations, you have to have your proverbial house in order—admin is critical for that. I spent almost as much time on the bridge navigating as I did in the admin office administrating. The exposure to that side of running a ship with the Executive Officer was a really great opportunity to peek behind the curtain and see how decisions were made from manning to legal to the ranking of Sailors and officers at enlisted evaluation (eval) and officer fitness report (FITREP) time. Getting administration and correspondence right is a critical skill and one that, with the advent of emails and virtual platforms, is quickly diminishing across the Navy. From navigation to admin, "attention to detail is the key to success." Mike said that to me over a beer when we had a port visit in Singapore on my first deployment.

11

Fair in the Channel*

Someone once said, "Experience is what you end up with when you screw up." That is certainly true *if* you learn from your mistakes. You have to recognize and accept that you messed up and put measures in place so you don't make the same mistake twice. For most of this book so far, I've shared what I didn't do right, so I think you could find it useful to know the things that I did do right. Things that got me fair in the channel.

I Love a Whiteboard

I was relatively organized as a Cadet—at least, organized when it came to keeping track of my weekends and penalty tours. I did maintain a running to-do list for homework assignments, term papers, hops, mixers, events, and others, but it was not nearly the quality organizational skills I developed for myself

---

* In navigational terms, this means you are in the center of the channel in safe water.

on the ship and have maintained ever since.

The bane of my existence at Surface Warfare Officers School Division Officer Course—or SWOSDOC (today it is the Basic Division Officers Course—BDOC)—was learning the maintenance and material management, or 3M system. The program management instruction was affectionately called "The Blue Bomber." For weeks, we were provided pretty detailed instruction in class on the sections. It was usually after lunch, and it was really hard to stay awake. So, as intrepid Ensigns, we took The Blue Bomber home and conducted study sessions together in a back room at the Irish American Athletic Club, which was conveniently within walking distance from our condo in Newport. And these sessions were usually conducted over a couple of pitchers of beer. Maybe the section on 3M would have been better learned without the beer, but that is insight gained with age. More to the point, though, what does this have to do with being organized on the ship? Everything. Your division will plan its week, month, and quarter based on the 3M scheduling system for all your equipment. Each piece of gear or equipment you and your division are responsible for is covered in the 3M system, including when you have to conduct maintenance and what type of maintenance. And it all must be completed. This is on top of all the cleaning, repairing, and operating of your equipment on a routine and operational basis.

We used to map out the maintenance checks on a paper quarterly board (a scheduling board like a calendar broken out into quarters) in pencil and, once approved, transcribe the weekly checks to a laminated weekly board in the work center with a grease pencil. Now it is all done via a computer program called SKED 3.0, which does a lot of the research and work for you when determining what checks need to be done and when. One of the biggest complaints you will get from your Sailors is "last-minute tasking." Much of that can be avoided by ensuring you, your Chief, and your leading petty officers (LPOs) are on top of this scheduling tool, planning the next week's maintenance on Thursday, and presenting it to your Sailors on Friday before they head off for the weekend.

I am a big believer in the whiteboard. When I had first and second division on my first ship, the LSD, we had two big whiteboards in the sail loft. First, we segmented off with tape and made a weekly job synchronization matrix on one board. In each block, we inscribed who was doing what, where it was being done, about how long we expected it to take, and who was the petty officer in charge (POIC). On the other board, we created two matrices and had a monthly and quarterly look at the long-term projections of our big jobs (e.g., painting the sides of the ship) overlaid with the big 3M planned maintenance jobs (e.g., semiannual or annual jobs like slushing the luff wire of the twenty-ton crane) that took a big chunk of people to accomplish. That way, we could prioritize jobs and people appropriately. We also included other big items like ship underways, training periods, inspections, certifications, and events that we would need to synchronize or deconflict with other departments. It was magic. And it was completely transparent to whoever walked into the space. The Sailors knew exactly what they needed to do and could plan ahead for things like days off, leave, or figuring out what they could get done and pull ahead to leave the ship early on Friday. We, as leaders and managers, knew where our folks were at any given time, who needed mentoring and supervision, and who was becoming a really good POIC.

My Sailors were happy and motivated, and our production skyrocketed. I still use a whiteboard, but Excel spreadsheets are really great for building these tools today.

Being Professionally Curious

When I came into the Navy, all ships stood three-section duty when we were in port—whether we were overseas or not. This was to support getting the ship underway with short notice or fighting a main space fire. Also, unmarried E-4s and below were required to live onboard the ship. Those were the requirements, and we really didn't think much of them because we didn't know any better.

I was very aggressive in knocking my quals out because, as I mentioned earlier, I really didn't intend on remaining a SWO. I was all over the ship when the day was done, and I wasn't standing watch. More often than not, I would end up in one of the engineering shops chatting with the guys who were onboard, or in the duty section. One of my favorite hangouts was the machine shop on the LSD. The HTs and MRs were a hoot, and they were always welding or brazing something— mostly they were practicing, but there was always some sort of competition. One evening, an MR1 asked me if I wanted to learn to weld and braze—uh, yeah, I did! I spent weeks learning the techniques and secrets to a good weld or braze (which is, of course, the preparation of the metal—clean and scuffed). I was also offered the opportunity to get qualified on the rough terrain (RT) forklift. I spent hours driving it around the well deck, up the ramp, and through the truck tunnel, and drifting around the flight deck (well, not really, just going in slow circles). I knocked out my PQS and was qualified to drive it.

As we were getting ready to get underway for our INSURV material inspection, we in E-Division were conducting checks on our sixty-ton crane. We had help from the folks at the Shore Intermediate Maintenance Activity (SIMA)—these were Sailors who were on shore duty honing their skills repairing ships on the waterfront. In this case, we were getting some tuning assistance with the crane motors from the electrician shop. The sixty-ton crane has access doors that open in between the arms of the crane. Running up the inside of the boom arms is the cabling for the lights, horn, and limit switches. The SIMA folks finished their work and left without telling us. When the boatswain's mates, who operated the crane, swung the crane over to lower the boom back into the cradle, we discovered the doors had been left open, which severed the cabling. This was a really big deal (and another lesson in here as an aside: always check someone else's homework if they leave it for you to act on). The CO was understandably angry and told me to get it fixed, and he didn't care how.

My guys and I looked at the mess of cables, and we discussed how we were going to replace the entire runs of the cables, where we needed to find cabling, and how we were going to get it all done—after 17:00 on a Monday. Then my EM1 had a brilliant idea. Why don't we just put a junction box where the cables were cut and only replace the cabling closest to the crane house? It was an elegant fix to a challenging problem. The issue was that we didn't have any HTs in the duty section, and the area where we needed to place the junction box was pretty high up. Back then, we didn't have cell phones to recall whomever we wanted.

So, I made a quick Ensign decision. I would drive the RT up, place a pallet on the forks to stand on, and grab the portable welding kit to weld the box inside the arm. My guys said, "Brilliant!" Well, they didn't say that. It was more along the lines of, "This isn't going to end well. The Divo is going to die." At any rate, we drove on.

While on his way home, the CO felt bad for yelling at me and decided to come back to the ship to see what could be done. By the time he made it back up to the flight deck, he found that the RT was in place, and someone was already welding the box. He found my EM1 and asked what we were doing. He explained everything, and the CO was really happy. He looked around and then asked where I was—EM1 just pointed. To say he was not really happy about an Ensign driving the RT and welding is a bit of an understatement. But he was super proud of how we addressed the problem and were self-reliant enough to get it fixed with no fanfare. I also had to produce all my quals for him the next day. The crane was fixed, and I think that box is still there today.

The point is that your professional curiosity can lead to knowledge and experience that has the potential to "save the day." Never pass up the opportunity to learn about things that may appear to be outside of your "swim lane." In this case, because of our divisional collective creativity, my professional curiosity to learn skills outside my division, and the application of those skills—and frankly, an aggressive approach to problem-solving—we genuinely saved the day.

A Natural . . .

When I was at SWOSDOC in Newport, Rhode Island, we had the opportunity to go out and practice ship-driving on the bay in the yard patrol boats, or YPs. They don't do that anymore outside of the Naval Academy. We had the opportunity to conduct underways from the pier and pier landings, underway replenishment (UNREP) approaches, or "leap frogs," station-keeping, and tactical divisional maneuvering (DIVTACs). I loved every minute of it.

When I got to my first ship, the premier shiphandler and designated new Ensign ship-driving mentor was a CWO4 and our ship's Electronic Maintenance Officer, or EMO. He was *really* good. My first sea and anchor detail (when you get the ship underway from a pier or anchorage or take the ship from sea into an anchorage or pier) was getting underway from Naval Station San Diego and putting out to sea. EMO and I talked on Friday about how we were going to do it, the engine combinations, line handling sequence, and how to use the tugs. I listened and asked questions. All throughout the weekend, I thought about how I was going to do it.

I remember my first sea and anchor detail like it was yesterday. It started out a little gray and foggy, but as the sun came up on that Monday morning, the fog burned off quickly. I was up on the bridge early and took note of the winds from the telltales on the cranes at the foot of the pier and the ship's anemometer, as well as the current from the ripples coming off the buoys in the channel and under the pier pilings. We were moored bow in, portside to, and had a Leahy-class cruiser moored behind us at the head of the pier. I had an offsetting current (the tide was coming in) at about 1.5 to 2 knots and a light onsetting breeze coming from the south at about 5 knots. Perfect. It is important to note that while wind plays a really important role in the factors that affect the ship, current is the strongest factor (one knot of current has the same effect as 30 knots of wind).

Somewhere in the South Pacific, 1997

We set sea and anchor detail just before 08:00, and the tugs came alongside. We made up (or connected) the tugs, but they did not take a strain, meaning they didn't pull on us or help us. I didn't really want to use them, and EMO agreed that we didn't need them. Using a combination of engines, lines, and rudder, we eased the stern away from the pier (starboard engine ahead 1/3, left full rudder), and we took in all lines but the bow line to use as a spring. As the stern started to swing out, I shifted the rudder and gave the order to reverse both engines at a 2/3 bell, and we took in the bow line. We used the current to gently take us away from the pier, and I used offsetting engine orders to straighten the bow, and then I used a 2/3 backing bell to get us out into the channel. Once the stern cleared the piers, I put my rudder over to right full, and the bow started to inch around to port. EMO and I agreed that we needed the tug to nudge our bow around a little quicker to get us fair in the channel. Once we did that, I came up to 1/3 ahead, cast off the tugs, and started up the channel.

It was a beautiful San Diego day by 08:00. We steamed up the harbor toward the Coronado Bay Bridge. I overheard the CO ask EMO how I did, and his response was, "This guy is either really good, or he is completely lost and got lucky. But I think he is a natural."

When we were clear of the channel and heading to Gasoline Alley to meet up with our oiler for an UNREP, we secured the sea and anchor detail and set the underway watch. EMO took me out on the bridgewing to debrief the transit. He asked what I thought. I said, "It was okay, but I messed up a few of my orders to the helm and lee helm. I was a little too fast coming out of the berth, and I lost track of a couple of contacts before they were passed and opening."

He said, "Well, yes, I agree with most of what you are saying, and you might be a little hard on yourself, which is fine. Tell me how you prepared for this morning." I told him about what I thought of over the weekend: getting up to the bridge early, observing the environment, and thinking through the process. He said, "You are my new favorite Ensign." As he turned and walked away, he said over his shoulder, "Great job this morning. You set your bar high. Now you have to maintain that bar and see if you can raise it even higher."

I love being at sea, and I love driving ships. Feeling the pitch and roll of the deck under your feet and the sea breeze and sun on your face is simply awesome. Add to that the amount of firepower and combat capability you have at your disposal, and you are in charge of, well, you just cannot replicate that anywhere. It is an awesome responsibility that hits you in the gut in the middle of the night as you are standing bridge watch—the hundreds of Sailors asleep in their racks trusting YOU with their lives. I am completely comfortable with that, and I am really good at it. You will be, too.

12

Navy Culture—
The Navy Is NOT VMI

This is obvious, right? Well, not always. I offer you a few thoughts on this unexpected twist.

If you thought going to VMI was a culture shock, welcome to the rest of your life (if you choose it to be). I struggled with my transition out of VMI and into the Navy. When I showed up to SWOSDOC in Newport, Rhode Island, in the summer of 1993, I was a man on a mission—not to study my rear off in SWOS but to enjoy to the fullest my newfound freedom and party the summer away. So, I very quickly ended up on academic probation. Not only did I not get to party as much as I wanted, but my newfound freedom was curtailed, and it was almost like being in barracks confinement again—staying in my apartment in Newport in the summer. What an ass clown.

When you get to your first duty station, make sure you temper your approach to your newfound freedom. I did eventually knuckle down, and I finished up not quite at the bottom of my class but nowhere near the top. Know this, too: Your professional reputation starts the minute you show up at your first duty station. I was lucky we didn't have email or anything like that back in the day—the first report on me would have done me in.

Contracting, 1992, with Col. John Ripley (USMC)

The Navy is not as military as VMI is. You will be used to a system of life that is very regimented and schedule-oriented, and you pretty much always have a place to be. Aside from a few daily meetings on the ship (which will increase in frequency the more senior you get), as a Divo, you won't have much that you HAVE to do. But there is a lot that you SHOULD be doing (e.g., quals, admin, checking in on your Sailors, quals, reviewing message traffic, professional development, quals, did I mention quals?). So, your day is predominantly yours in port. Underway, you will have a bit more structure with your watch-standing schedule, but again, your time is really yours to use constructively or yours to waste.

With your spare time, you should aggressively knock out your quals. You need to set aside time in your day to take care of your Sailors and circulate where they are working to make sure they have what they need.

Navy people yelling at you is not nearly as intimidating as Cadre or the RDC. They just aren't. A few of my COs were really frustrated that they could not get in my head or make me flustered when they got on my ass about things. My VMI ROTC Professor of Naval Science, Col. John Ripley, was a legend in the Marine Corps, a Vietnam War legend, and a Navy Cross recipient, so he got in my head when he chewed my ass. Most of my leadership out in the fleet just didn't strike that chord with me. Once, when I was being "talked to," I was accused of looking bored. That did not go well and just extended the ass-chewing. Try not to look bored when the DH/XO/CO is yelling at you.

Conversely, you might be really talented at flame-spraying* Rats and Thirds, but applying that same approach to your Sailors all the time is not going to work. As noted earlier, "dinner theater" has its time and place, but yelling all the time makes you look weak and stupid. Your Sailors are not Rats—don't treat them that way.

As a VMI-trained officer, you have certain credibility. If you find yourself working with the Marines or with our sister services, your credibility gets bumped up a notch. We've worked very hard to foster that over the years. Don't muck it up, and don't forget where you came from.

And no one understands VMI-speak in the fleet—there just aren't that many of us. So, when you find each other, it is magic.

---

* Flame-spraying in VMI parlance is yelling at someone.

Chance meeting with a Brother Rat, 1996

Because we are so few in the fleet, we older VMI alumni are proud of you and proud to serve alongside you. Never be afraid to shake the hand of a fellow alum (either senior or junior) and introduce yourself.

Bravo Company is still the best company on the Hill.

But . . .

There is always a "but," right?

While the Navy isn't VMI, there are lots of things that do translate well. Here are a few things I think VMI instilled in me that have helped me as a JO and, really, throughout my entire career.

The Honor System. You'd think this is an obvious one, but sadly, it isn't. We are known for our honor code, and by and large, it is expected of you wherever you go. I've seen officers straight up lie to their department head, the XO, and the CO. When I screwed up, I fessed up immediately and told my boss what I was going to do to fix it. When I was the navigator of an FFG, we were making a transit from Japan to Hawaii. I charted our course and sent our transit plan to Seventh Fleet for approval. My guys looked at it, Ops looked at it, the XO looked at it, and the CO looked at it. Everyone agreed it was solid, and we sent it off. But, when I pulled the message out of traffic, something looked weird. I looked at it for a couple of days—then it hit me. I completely forgot to take into account the international date line. But everyone looked at the plan, right? Sure, they looked at it, but they trusted me, my experience, and my expertise—no one even considered I'd jack it up. I went straight to the CO and said, "I screwed this up." He actually laughed.

He said, "I guess you want to cancel the first message and send a new one, right? You know, everyone will see your mistake. You okay with that?" I said sure. He told me to go ahead and fly the amended message. Which I did. Later, he said that we probably didn't need to send the message and that we could have just fudged the speed across the transit to make it all work out, which had crossed my mind, but it wasn't honest. I did get a ration of grief for it from the DESRON commodore, but he also said that we could have fudged the speed across the transit and it really wouldn't have mattered.

My CO said to him, "Of course it matters to Nav. He is a VMI guy." I am also a professional, and I am trusted.

Time management. As a Cadet, you know exactly when you need to wake up to give yourself enough time to get up, get dressed, and walk out to your specific spot in formation or to your class. Down to the second. This translates into getting to meetings on time, making your watch rotation on time, and many others.

Sucking it up. VMI is a great place to be from, but not always a great place to be. We all get it. But what you are willing to put up with and muscle through is far more than what most of your peers are willing to deal with. Many will roll over and show their bellies in defeat when you are just getting warmed up. VMI—never say die.

The VMI Arc of Experience. As an Ensign reporting to your ship, you will see echoes and shades of VMI. When you report to your first ship, you are basically a Rat again (albeit without the hazing and shenanigans—sort of). You are learning a new environment, figuring out the ins and outs of the wardroom, and learning your jobs. Then, after a bit, you become a Third. The newness of it wears off, some new Ensigns report, and then everyone ignores you until they recognize you aren't SWO qualified yet and people start busting your chops—you will continue to eat shit. Then you become a Second. The minute you get your SWO pin, your life changes. Everything is awesome, and somehow you are respectable and looked up to. As you end your first tour, you become a First, the "wise" old LTjg who has passed through the trials and tribulations of SWO qualification; you are an old pro at running your division, and you are mentoring those who are just showing up. You know and should recognize the process—except you are now pulling a real paycheck and you don't have to go back to barracks— unless you are on deployment, and then yes, you have to go back to barracks.

13

Rapid-Fire Memes

Over the years, I've heard sayings from bosses that stuck with me, and I've internalized them. We call these sayings maxims: short statements that convey a general truth or rule of conduct. Today, you might call them serious memes. Some were motivational, some were admonitions, and some were just spot-on observations. But all of them have applications across the spectrum of what we do as warfighters. I like them because they are easy to remember and can deliver a very powerful message in a clear and concise manner. I intended on writing only a few, but there are so many of them that I picked my favorites. Here they are.

Expect What You Inspect

A favorite of my fourth-ship CO, this one is pretty self-explanatory and applicable to everything we do, which is why I put it first. Don't expect something to turn out the way you want it to if you don't inspect the progress through to completion.

During one of my first zone inspections on my first ship, I walked around my E-Division spaces with the First Lieutenant. I figured it would be a breeze because he wasn't an engineer; it was a Friday, everyone just wanted this inspection to be over with, and I gave clear guidance to my division on space preparation for the inspection. What was supposed to be a quick walk-around turned out to be a disaster. When First and I walked around, I discovered the spaces were not what I expected them to be. Some were cluttered and dirty, some were still locked and we couldn't go in, and some hadn't been touched at all. First gave me a long and condescending lecture on how to do inspections, how to prepare for inspections, and how we were going to reinspect the following week. I was furious and embarrassed. When I went to roll in hot on my division, they had already left for liberty. I called them back in and read them the riot act.

While standing duty that Sunday, I was lamenting my findings with the main propulsion assistant (MPA), who was a warrant officer. He asked if I walked around prior to the inspection with the zone inspection sheets (Zone Inspection Discrepancy List—or ZIDL) from the prior inspection. No. Did I walk around with my LPO and pre-inspect the spaces? No. Did I validate the list of spaces to be inspected with the zone inspection coordinator? No. Did you effectively task the division to get those spaces clean in enough time to get it all done? No. He said, "You owe your guys an apology for fucking up their Friday liberty. Their failure to prepare was your failure to provide oversight and direction." Lesson learned. Expect what you inspect.

Do Not Be Constrained by the Standard— Exceed It at All Opportunities

Don't let the standard become the goal or the finish line. Standards are established for a reason. Standards are the baseline for what we do. Anything produced or executed that is substandard will ultimately result in failure. Demand the standard, but encourage exceeding the standard. Once exceeding the standard becomes standard, you have established a culture of excellence.

Define, Refine, Execute

Define the requirement and the plan, refine the plan, and then execute the plan. You will always hear the naysayers in the background saying, "No plan survives first contact." This is true, but a defined plan that is understood by all allows for coordinated change if necessary. Because everyone knows clearly what the desired end goal is, refinements to the plan will enable continued convergence on the desired end state. And, finally, in execution, all players move forward in a coordinated fashion.

While much of what we do in peacetime is centered around maintenance and training, it is essential to recognize that the "plan," no matter what it is or for, is always focused on combat readiness. If your end goal is combat readiness, your plan must be understood by all—even at the divisional level. Combat readiness begins with meticulous planning to generate the material readiness required to support unencumbered, effective training and operational readiness that ultimately leads to a combat-ready team. In defining your plan, you must regressively plan: figure out the end state and work backward to the present day.

Be an Island of Calm in a Sea of Chaos

When things go sideways, and they will, this is what you need to do: Step back and take a deep breath, look around and assess the situation, decide your course of action, and act decisively. Stay calm and do not get caught up in the group churn. It will quickly devolve into panic, and panic is a deadly virus.

Air Force Colonel John Boyd came up with a process that enabled USAF fighter pilots to think faster than the adversary, which upset the adversary's process and approach to an engagement. This process is called the OODA loop. Observe, Orient, Decide, Act. It is a constant loop (which sometimes overlaps other loops) of decision-making. The enemy wants to get in your OODA loop and disrupt it—you want to do the same to them. This is where your foundation in tactics and doctrine will allow you to recover your loop quickly and outthink them.

In order for you to be that island of calm, you first have to establish your informational baseline. I established a physical loop on the bridge of a ship when I was the conning officer (Conn) and modified it later as an officer of the deck (OOD), and went on to establish the same thing in CIC as a tactical action officer (TAO). I would start at the centerline pelorus, walk over to the radar and plot the contacts as necessary, walk out to the bridgewing and see if what I saw on the radar matched what I was seeing visually, then walk to the other bridgewing and do the same, and then walk back to the centerline. Nothing ever stays static at sea—everything changes every second. You must have the complete picture to make quick decisions. As you make your observations, you orient yourself to be able to proceed to the next event, like changing position in a formation or responding quickly to an unexpected casualty. This data will facilitate your swift decision-making as situations develop. With the basis of your cycle complete, you can close the loop and act decisively and smartly.

On my first deployment, we were heading home south through the Strait of Malacca. This is one of the busiest and most constrained straits on the planet—if you are not doing twenty knots or something close to that, you are going to get run over. There is very little room to maneuver throughout most of the transit, and it is super stressful. As we were making our transit around midday, I had the watch as the conning officer. The CO had been on the bridge for a few hours, as had the XO and a few of the department heads. As one of the A-Team conning officers, I had been on the bridge since we started the transit. I was to be relieved at the halfway mark, and I had a few hours left.

We reached a point in the transit where we had only a few hundred yards to our starboard to shoal water and a few hundred yards to port to the northbound traffic. Now, all sorts of ships make this passage, including local tramp steamers. One of the major industries in Southeast Asia is lumber. Some of the logs that are transported via water are absolutely monstrous—as big around as a bus. Two of those logs must have fallen off a local steamer and were floating ahead of us. They appeared to be astride our side of the channel and almost arranged end to end, just a few hundred yards ahead. The CO and I saw them at the same time. This is where my loop paid off. Because I had a really good idea of all the traffic that was aside and behind us and now a better picture of what was ahead, I knew I had only one way to go. I knew we had only a full bell rung up and had some room to goose it. I had to make a decision to go, so I calmly decided to call up a flank bell and try to split the difference between the logs.

The CO realized what I was doing and was about to countermand the order when he realized we really had no other choice. I gave steering orders to the helm, meaning not a course to steer but to adjust the rudder and steady on my commands. The logs appeared to be closing in on each other as we approached them. As the ship slowly gained speed, the bow wave that was created was enough to push the logs out, just enough for us to squeeze through. As we passed the logs, the CO ran to one bridgewing and I to the other, and we saw that we cleared the logs by scant feet. I strode back into the bridge and over the bridge-to-bridge radio, warning the ship that was right behind us about the logs.

The CO asked afterward, "You knew that was going to work, right?"

I said, "I took a few seconds to assess everything I knew. I knew where everyone was; I knew how much room I had to port, starboard, ahead, and astern; I knew where my engines were and what I had to work with; and I am comfortable with the handling of the ship. So sure, I was confident it would work." By being able to maintain my situational awareness and constantly updating my decision-making data, I could make a rapid and decisive decision, not in haste but with speed. That is what being on that island of calm is all about—but don't forget to continuously cultivate your island.

Leadership Is Hard

There is nothing easy about leadership. Sometimes, we have to make unpopular but necessary decisions. Not everyone will agree with or like your decision. If you know it is the right thing to do, no matter how hard or unpopular, you must have the courage and conviction to do the right thing.

As a Division Officer, the decisions that reside in your wheelhouse will most likely affect just you and your division. Deciding to put your folks on liberty, deciding to put the extra time in on PMS, inspecting spaces post-sweepers, and calling people back into work for jobs not completed or completed incorrectly. These are the decisions that will define your character, manage expectations both up and down the chain of command, and set your foundation for years to come. At the same time, however, you can make mistakes—that is okay as long as you own your mistakes and learn from them.

Referring back to the "expect what you inspect" story, I took a face shot from the Chief Engineer, who yelled at me a bit and finished up by saying, "Your spaces still suck."

My response was the only one that I could give: "Aye, sir. My fault." Later, I got in front of my division and expressed my lament for not setting expectations, following up with them, and ruining their Friday. I did not get a rousing "It's okay, boss!" but I did get the public acknowledgment from my first classes that they could have done better as well. We all learned from the event and got better from then on. What I got privately from the first classes was that they were actually glad I called them all back and held the division to a standard. They were glad that they had a leader who was not afraid to make tough calls. They also respected that I took the responsibility and didn't throw the division under the bus. They had heard from the MPA that I took the ass-chewing and never shifted any blame.

Leaders lead from the front, so it is fitting and right that you take the face shot for your folks. You can't lead from behind.

Never Quit; Failure Is Okay, but If You Quit, You Will Never Learn from a Failure

VMI—we never say die.

A Little Pain Never Hurt Nobody

My high school swimming coach was fond of this one. Not everything is going to go your way—everyone has a bad day. Get over it; no one cares. It just makes you stronger and more resilient.

In this day and age of mental wellness, this might come across as flippant. Believe me, it is not. You have to learn to recognize what is truly an emotional event and what is just a bad day. As a leader, though, you need to not only take care of your Sailors and recognize when they need help, but also recognize it in yourself and have the courage to ask for help when you need it. It is not an act of weakness to ask for help—it shows maturity and strength.

Operations Are Executed at the Speed of the Proficiency of the Watch Stander

Ensure your watch team is trained and meets your expectations. Inspect and engage your folks every time you take a watch—every watch will be a learning and/or teaching opportunity. Your team is a reflection of you. If it sucks, so do you. You need to make sure your team has the tools and training it needs to execute its tasks, from sea and anchor detail to a complex, live missile engagement.

Always think through "what-if" scenarios in your head and anticipate what you will do. Your immediate and controlling actions will determine the outcome of a potentially dangerous situation. The key to speed is practice, practice, practice. I used to make my watch teams talk through man-overboards, loss of steering, low visibility, and other drills on the bridge every single watch—a mid-watch can get really boring, but engaging the team will make them alert and sharp. I did the same in CIC and in engineering (although the engineers usually have scheduled evolutions and drills already baked into the watch). You never want the first time your team does something to be the first time for real.

This Ship Is Built to Fight.
You Had Better Know How*

If you don't know who said this, you need to get into your naval heritage. This is one of the most important takeaways from this book. *Learn to fight your ship*. Understand the combat systems and how they all interact, and how your ship, as a member of a destroyer squadron or strike group, is a part of a kill chain that is designed to defeat the enemy. The enemy has already studied you and thought about how they will kill you. Along with the technical know-how of how the combat system works, learn doctrine and tactics, so when it counts, you can creatively disrupt the enemy's plan and then kill them with the utmost violence. We've given you the tools; you just need to know how to use them.

---

* Admiral Arleigh Burke said this in his remarks to the crew of the newly commissioned USS *Arleigh Burke* (DDG-51)—the first of its class.

14

A Few Words of Caution

Check Your Ego at the Door

Ruthless self-assessment is critical to establishing a culture of excellence to enable combat readiness. If you and your division suck, acknowledge it and make a plan to get it right. Be data-driven, foster ruthless self-assessment, and anticipate inspections and assessments.

If every bit of criticism is going to wear on your confidence, your motivation, and your sense of self, you are in for a rude awakening. I love the aviator way of debriefs. They are blunt and to the point—if you jacked up an event, it is broken down into minute detail as to how you messed it up. This method gets straight to the most important point: learning. That open atmosphere is conducive to constructive criticism, and everyone learns. I have observed over the years that we SWOs are not really good at this at all. We are not good at providing open criticism of an event, and we are not good at receiving that criticism—our egos are too easily bruised. We need to be better at this to get better.

We Are Not as Good as We Think We Are (Or as Good as Our Reputation)

I was on a ship that had a phenomenal reputation on the waterfront as the Gold Standard. In reality, the ship barely performed to standard. But we thought we were awesome. It was all smoke and mirrors based on the CO's personality and bullying of the assessors and certifiers. As I looked under the bonnet, it was an ugly baby. Over time, we recognized and accepted that we were not awesome and had a lot of room for improvement, and we began to work on *earning* our reputation. Which we did, and then *exceeded it*. Ensure you self-reflect and are honest in your self-assessment. If you don't like what you find, fix it.

Hitting "Send" on an Email Does Not Imply Action Complete

This maxim is pretty self-explanatory: you must follow up. Hitting send on a completed email-tasker or direction to subordinates with a resounding "click" on the mouse feels good. The issue with this tends to be that the receiver, or receivers, have follow-up questions and sometimes don't understand your task. You've generated more questions than answers. Always make sure you follow up with your recipient to make sure you've met the mark. This also relates back to expecting what you inspect.

Soak Time

This may seem to be a little above the pay grade of the Division Officer, but your presence on the deckplates (or where your Sailors are working) will give you great insight on the status of your Sailors. You need to be mindful of their well-being, mental state, and general health. It seems intuitive, but it is harder to discern than it sounds. During the ship's training phases, this is an especially important aspect to pay close attention to. As you assess your Sailors, you need to be cognizant of the impacts of the operational tempo (OPTEMPO) of training, maintenance, and operations. Your input and observations up the chain of command will be taken into account. However, the corollary to that is that you have to trust that the chain of command is managing that rheostat mindfully. We surface warriors cannot afford to be one-trick ponies, but during training it is necessary to manage pace in order to not exhaust the crew, not create a self-defeating schedule, and ensure there is enough time between events to rest, recover, and reflect. Rest the crew, recover the equipment, and allow reflection time to enable the lessons of the training to sink in: soak time. Trying to do too many things at the same time in very quick succession may check all the boxes, but it does not lay solid foundations for tactical and operational success. Well-thought-out, paced, and executed training evolutions will facilitate multitasking when you are integrated and enable you to balance multiple threats simultaneously. If your Sailors are harried and exhausted and their equipment does not work, all the training will be for naught.

You Can Fake Interest, but You Can't Fake Being There

I worked with a guy who always seemed to be fussing about his paperwork, his schedule, his work lists, and the whereabouts of the Sailors in his division. He would always be quickly walking around the ship with an angry look on his face and carrying a clipboard full of papers and messages. Don't get in his way, or you'll get run over. He seemed to always be interested in what was going on. One day, we thought we'd mess with him and hide his clipboard during lunch. My job was to get it and hide it while the other guys kept him distracted. In my haste to hide the paper-holding monstrosity, I dropped it. The top couple of sheets were actual messages and lists, but the rest of the ream of paper was blank. This got me thinking. Then—not that I had nothing better to do—I decided to follow him around. And follow him around, and around, and around I did. He went nowhere but in circles around the ship. But he looked busy—and he was telling everyone he was doing things for his division. His Sailors suffered because he was never where they needed him, and he never really provided them with any leadership or guidance. Be there for your Sailors when they need you—you will recognize it when the time comes.

Liberty–It Is a Mission

Make sure you get out and see stuff on deployment. I reflected on my first deployment when I got home and realized I hadn't seen much except the inside of a bunch of pubs. And a lot of that was pretty hazy. Do not discount the MWR tours—they are awesome, inexpensive, and, more often than not, geared toward your age group. When I got to my second ship, I made a promise to myself to go and see "culture and local stuff" (i.e., landmarks, tours, good local restaurants) before I met up with my buddies at the bars. Get out into the country you are visiting and take in the culture; go and see a museum; take a tour; or get lost in the local atmosphere before you partake in some cultured libations. I still like to head off and explore with only a general direction in mind—you never know what you will find or what cool experience awaits you. Some of my most cherished liberty memories were chance encounters.

With full transparency, though, I wouldn't have made it past Lieutenant Junior Grade if we had cell phones with cameras and social media back in the day. For better or worse, fleet liberty policies (those rules laid down by the fleet commanders that determine what you can and cannot do on your time off in foreign ports) are more restrictive now than they were when I was in your shoes. What you do on liberty can end up on some social media feed literally in the blink of an eye. This is why we say now that liberty is a mission—and it is really a no-fail mission. But you can and should still go out and have fun. On my last few deployments, and mind you, even the senior guys like to go out and tear it up every now and again, I made sure my cell phone did not come out of my pocket, and we always went out with a plan that included getting back to the ship on time and in one piece.

We All Know the Navy Is Never Wrong, but Sometimes It Is a Little Short of Being Right

COs and bosses in general are all unique, and your approach to them is your responsibility. In the P-XO pipeline at SWOS, we were always told, "If you have a personality conflict with your CO, he or she has the personality; you have the conflict. Figure it out." You have the obligation in the senior/subordinate relationship to try to steer the boss down the channel—even when they seem to be dead set on a course of action. There are a few things that you must stand firm on: safety, ethics, morals, and legality; everything else is pretty negotiable.

Your Sailors Are NOT Your Friends

I hope you come to love your Sailors—in the right sense of the word (i.e., not fraternization). I got really close to my first division—too close.

Many of your Sailors will be around your age and have many common interests. I spent a lot of time with my guys and learned what they did. I also went out with my Sailors to some of the local pubs in San Diego. My Sailors were exceptionally loyal—we were friends. This is BAD.

When going through the training cycle, I was a repair locker officer and was being observed by an assessor. That assessor was a damage control senior Chief who pulled me aside after one drill. He asked how many of my teammates were from my division, and I had about five—a little heavy. I thought I stacked my locker with people I could trust and depend on. He saw that I stacked my locker with people I liked. He said, "Your Sailors will do anything you ask, immediately—which is great. But you like them too much. You will have to make a decision to send a couple of them into a burning room or flooded space because you know their actions will save the ship, but they will likely die. They might not hesitate, but you will. Your hesitation will jeopardize the four hundred lives on this ship. You cannot hesitate. These Sailors are NOT your friends."

It is a tough lesson, but a necessary one.

Put on Your CO Goggles

When I was XO of a DDG, my CO used to say, "Put on my goggles and see things from my perspective when making your XO decisions." Sometimes it is tough to see the bigger picture when you are mired in your own divisional or organizational challenges. But it is important to remember that in large organizations, the guy at the top has to look at all the challenges across the organization and prioritize which ones are the most important at the time. When you look through your own goggles, your problem may seem huge, but through the goggles of the boss, your problem is not at the top of his or her priority list.

What We Have Here Is a Failure to Communicate

I had a boss who used to say, "The greatest staff sin is a failure to cross-communicate." You can exchange the word staff for work center, division, department, or wardroom. This happens more often than we'd like to admit, and it kills me. Unfortunately for you and your fellow JOs, this is one that you will always learn the hard way. It is so simple, yet it is one of the most common failures in our organization—usually caused by sheer laziness. If you don't coordinate across an organization, you are destined to fail. Your well-thought-out plan will immediately hit resistance when someone else has an equally well-thought-out plan that conflicts with yours. Don't let a failure to communicate result in multiple failures. Likewise, decisions you make for yourself and your division might have an impact across the organization at large. You need to be aware of those potential impacts.

Be a Rock-Turner

When you get to your first ship, the reasonable expectation is that everything is functioning as it should. You should look at the ship and your division metaphorically as a field of rocks. If you've ever been hiking and come across a field strewn with rocks, your initial impression is that they don't look out of place. Grass grows up around them; they've settled into the dirt, and most just peek up above the dirt or grass. Beneath those rocks could hide treasures or problems. It is rare to find treasure. Look for the problems—do not settle for what you see in front of you and take it for granted. Make sure to turn the rocks over. Nothing is perfect, and everything you find can be made better. No division, department, or ship is perfect; there is always room to improve. Your goals should always slant toward a continuous improvement process.

Don't Bring Me Problems, Bring Me Solutions

You will run into issues that you can't solve, and you will need a decision or direction from the boss. But don't just show up in their office with your problem and no ideas on how to fix it. Bring them your problem, but bring a plan, too. Also, don't attach your ego to your plan. When someone senior to you changes or dismisses your plan, don't sweat it. It is not worth the agony. What is important, and what gets noticed, is that you even came up with a plan. At least you thought through the problem and offered a solution. It might not be what the boss goes with, but they will appreciate your thought process.

There is a bit of a corollary to this, however. Offer your boss the opportunity to participate in the solution. Make sure you include the boss in big decisions, or even small ones if you think the boss needs to know. It is rare that any CO or leader will squash you for over-informing. The XO might dial your rheostat down a bit, but you never want to hear, "Why didn't you tell me when you knew?"

The Command Takes on the Personality of Its Commander

I firmly believe this one—from the Division Officer up to the CO of the ship. As noted above, your people are a direct reflection of you and your leadership. From the movie *Remember the Titans*, "Attitude reflects leadership." This is so true. If you don't care, neither will your Sailors. They will emulate your attitude, your priorities, and your personality. And always remember, there is some Seaman Timmy or Sally out there who looks at you and wants to be you someday. That is a massive responsibility; don't let them down. Set the standard, meet the standard, and exceed the standard. Your Sailors will follow your lead to the point that they will do what you want of them before you even ask—if you do it right.

Understand the Process, Read Instructions, and Make the Documentation Work for You

Like the Blue Book,* make the rules work for you. You don't need to be the barracks lawyer, but understanding the instructions and guidance makes you better informed to make the right decisions. You can make Navy publications and instructions work for you. Many are written vaguely for a reason—to allow the operational commander space to interpret the instruction.

---

* The Blue Book at VMI is a collection of rules and regulations that govern just about everything, from things as simple as tying your shoes and how to arrange your locker to how an inspection is to be conducted and the proper method of wearing a certain uniform.

It is up to you to read and understand an instruction or manual and to understand the decision space that is between the lines of the text.

This Is the Easiest Job in the World

Broken down for the Blueshirts (enlisted Sailors), I always tell them when they check in, "The Navy is one of the easiest jobs you may ever have. The secret to success lies in three things: show up on time, show up in the right uniform, and do what you are told." That's it; the rest of it will work itself out. It applies to Division Officers as well, but only for a short amount of time.

Daydreaming CAN Be Productive

Always think through "what-if" scenarios in your head and anticipate what you will do—your immediate and controlling actions will determine the outcome of a potentially dangerous situation.

Cultivate Your Spies

This sounds a little ominous and James Bond-ish, but it is much simpler than that. There will always be that one Sailor in your division who knows everyone, is well-liked, and has a good pulse on what is going on. Get to know that Sailor and make it a habit to chat them up. Really, you should be able to chat up all your Sailors, and you should get around and talk to all of them, but you need to figure out who will give you the straight talk.

There are also places where your Sailors will naturally collect and shoot the breeze. On my first ship, it was the battery shop when I had E-Division and the sail loft when I had first and second division. Lots of times, I would walk in and just listen to what was going on. You can gauge a lot by how your Sailors react when you walk into a space. Do they become immediately quiet and distant; do they acknowledge your presence and then get quiet; or do they acknowledge your presence and include you in the conversation? You will establish that rapport. But more to the point, listening is one of the key attributes to developing as a leader. Listen and sift the wheat from the chaff—find out what good kernels of information you can take from listening as opposed to the random rumors and things you really didn't need or want to hear.

The Efficacy of Dinner Theater

Losing your temper is akin to losing the battle. If you cannot control your emotions, then your folks will lose trust and confidence in you. Control your tongue and emotions. However, there may arise an occasion to demonstrate your Sally Port flame-spray. Use it very deliberately and sparingly. The dinner theater of a good ass-chewing will not be lost if you don't do it very often. And never cuss while doing it. Cursing makes you look ignorant.

On my first deployment, we pulled into Singapore. E-Division's responsibilities were simple: get hooked up to and aligned with shore power, then shift to shore power. Then we had to hook up the telephone lines. Back then, only the CO, XO, CMDCM, quarterdeck, Ops, and the engineering log room had access to international POTS (plain old telephone system) lines. The CO's line always got hooked up first and tested so they could call the bosses (whoever the fleet commander or immediate commander was, and the wife). On this particular afternoon, my guys hooked up the shore power cables, shifted to shore power, and went on liberty. We did not hook up the phone lines.

When I figured out we had forgotten the POTS lines (the CO asked, "Hey Erik, why doesn't my phone work?"), I went to find my IC men to get the lines hooked up, but they were all gone on liberty. So, I went to work with my functional but limited knowledge of the ship's telephone system.

I tossed the bundle of cable down from the deck of the ship to the pier and went down with the line diagram we got from the husbanding agent for the pier services. When I was at the box hooking up the lines, it started to rain. This was not just any rain; it was Singapore-in-the-summer rain, which meant solid sheets of water coming from the sky. I tested all the circuits at the pier, and they were all good. I even used the CO's line to call Mom and Dad for a few minutes just to make sure it worked. I figured it was justified because of all the tingles I got while hooking all the lines up.

When the lines were all hooked up, I went up to the quarterdeck to make sure it worked. And it did. Crisis averted—so I thought. I went up to the CO's cabin and told him that his line was good to go. I asked him if I could test it to make sure, and he said, "Don't bother." So, I went to eat dinner. Two bites in and over the 1MC, I heard, "Ensign Nilsson, your presence is requested in the commanding officer's cabin." Shit. I ran up to the CO's cabin, and the phone was dead. I told him how bad the rain was and that maybe some water intruded on the cabinet on the pier or on the ship, and that I'd have someone get to work on it. That someone was me.

By this time, it was dark, and I was reaching the extent of my knowledge of the IC circuits. I must have retraced the line three or four times (up and down all the ladders on and off the ship) and found nothing wrong with anything. It finally dawned on me to check the fuse in the phone junction box outside the CO's cabin. It turns out, it was bad.

As I was changing the fuse (with all my safety gear on this time), the CO walked out of the cabin. "Erik, what are you doing?" he asked.

I replied, "Changing the fuse, sir."

"Why you?" he asked. I guess the look on my face told him everything. He just said, "Let me know when you are done." And he walked back into his cabin. Two minutes later, the fuse was changed, and at 23:00, he had his phone access—five hours after I started this voyage of discovery.

Obviously, I was a bit angry. In fact, I was furious. To add insult to injury, I had the midnight to 04:00 watch on the quarterdeck. Plenty of time to stew and have the opportunity to see all my guys come gleefully across the quarterdeck having sampled the best beer in Singapore—Tiger Beer (and it really is good!). I also had the opportunity to realize that I never saw the duty section watch bill, and I had let my guys go without asking all the right questions. However, my senior enlisted leadership (all E-6s) did not validate that all the work had been done.

The next morning, we mustered for quarters. Our spot was at the aft end of the flight deck on the port quarter. That was the side that faced the harbor. We formed up adjacent to the marine formation. It was a typical hot and humid morning, and, coupled with the hangovers, it was pretty miserable. EM1 stepped up on my arrival, saluted, and stated, "E-Division, all present or accounted for."

I replied, "Very well—fall in."

I did not take them out of the position of attention, and in my best parade deck voice, I lit into them. "Who was responsible for the phone lines? Why did you all go on liberty without hooking them up? Where was the leadership? Where was the attention to detail? You left me here to figure this out all on my own! No thanks to you; our phones work! You call yourselves a division, NOPE! I am so disappointed in you that you don't even get to look at me—ABOUT FACE!" They all turned and faced the harbor. I continued to harangue them for the next five minutes about duty, professionalism, and loyalty. And then I chucked my clipboard over their heads into the harbor in a shower of paperwork. I turned and walked away.

The Marines remained frozen in position until I walked off the flight deck. After I left, the Gunnery Sergeant told my LPO that was the most epic but professional ass-chewing he'd ever witnessed. Evidently, they heard me all the way up on the O-5 level on the ship—a bit of a distance on an LSD.

My guys came up to me individually, apologized, and promised it would never happen again. And it never did. In fact, we never missed a deadline, gooned an inspection, or let our standards lax. Also, I never had to raise my voice again to E-Division.

15

Advice for Working with Senior Leaders

When I was an Ensign, I gave a brief during the arrival conference for our maintenance period at a shipyard. There were a number of senior leaders there, including the Commodore, the CO of the maintenance facility, and some senior civilians. I had to brief how we were shifting over from ship's power to shore power and the electrical distribution set up we would have during the yard period. I knew my system backward and forward. During the brief, the Chief Engineer, who was in charge of the entire yard period, interrupted me and tried to correct me on a system parameter I was discussing. He was wrong, and I corrected him very bluntly. It silenced the room. He was not happy, and it evidently surprised the leadership in the room. From my perspective, I showed everyone how well I knew my stuff. Fast forward a couple of years, and the next ship I was on was entering the same yard for maintenance. I recognized a few people in the room from the last time I was there. I had nothing to brief as I was the Navigator, but one of the senior civilians came up to me and the CO and asked if I was briefing. I said no, and he turned to the CO and said, "Good thing, this guy really knows how to silence a room." Not a great lasting impression.

As a junior officer, I would get so frustrated and a little outraged over the demands of senior officers, especially when it came to presenting to them or putting PowerPoint briefs together. Most times, leaders want you to get right to the point and get impatient with you as you are trying to explain something to them. In most senior-level briefs, you must use a certain font, a certain color, a certain design, and so on. It seemed overly particular or demanding from my point of view.

What I did not understand as a junior officer was the amount of information and detail that these leaders have to digest over the course of a day. Some leaders are presented with discussions over a day of meetings or see two or three briefs a day.* It is important to present your material in a fashion that they can easily digest. You would be surprised by the volume of information your leaders have to process every day. While your issue might be the most important thing on your plate, it might not rate that highly on your boss's plate. It is incumbent on you to present your boss with what we call "digestible bites," meaning you've already distilled the problem into what is wrong, what is needed, what your plan is, and what you need your boss to do. In order to do this, you need to: make sure your facts are

---

* There is a distinction between discussions and briefs. Meetings about specific topics are discussions, whereas briefs are formal presentations (usually in the form of a PowerPoint) that follow a certain agenda to present the boss with an idea, information, a concept of operations, or a number of courses of action from which to make a decision.

straight (and indeed facts, not tribal lore or hearsay); get to the point (only the CO gets to tell winding stories); stay consistent throughout your discussion; make sure you are aligned with policy (and if you are diverging, be clear as to why and the risks involved); be compelling in your discussion and be confident; and be credible—don't bullshit the boss.

It is important to know your audience. You have to take the time to get to know your leadership, how they like to receive information, how they like to process things, and how they want you to present. There is a bit of empathy that goes into this, as well as emotional intelligence. Once we worked for an admiral who had a couple of trigger words—things that would just set him off. Don't "poke the bear." If you know something triggers the boss, then just stay away from it, no matter how silly it may seem.

One of my bosses used to say, "Set the stage, raise the curtain." If there is some background information that is required to better understand the situation, make sure you bring it to light. But don't make it a voyage of discovery; just explain why this is important up front to put things in perspective. If whoever you are briefing is aware of what you are talking about, they will usually let you know and have you cut to the chase.

When you brief up the chain of command, it is usually a "reassurance brief." This means that the higher headquarters leadership probably already knows what you are doing, why you are doing it, and how you are doing it. What they want is to be reassured that you know what you are doing and to be told if you need any assistance from them. It's a simple concept, but you'd be surprised at how many people miss the mark on this—even at the flag level. At your level, it is probably a good guess that your leadership has seen your issue before and wants to see how you will handle it. Everything is a test.

You also want to try to get ahead of the boss—anticipate his or her direction. If you understand his or her intent and how he or she wants to operate, you enable freedom to maneuver within the organization, which enables efficiency and effectiveness. With most leaders, that is hard to do because they are typically experienced and may be way ahead of the staff. I worked for an admiral who was notoriously ahead of his staff, and it was always a sign of success when I heard him say, "Erik, would you please allow me the illusion of command?"

As a junior officer, your interaction with senior officers may be short and fleeting, but you want to put your best foot forward. Many times, a senior leader might want to know something about you before or after you begin. Make sure you have a quick thirty-second elevator speech about yourself. Be prepared, and do your prep work. If you are to be remembered, make it for a good reason.

16

The Day-to-Day Grind

Your day-to-day operations, especially on deployment, can seem like Groundhog Day—it all looks the same and it all runs together. Do not get complacent. It is not just a saying that everything can kill you on a ship at sea, because everything can kill you on a ship at sea. So, with that in mind, I offer a few things for you to consider.

Don't be surprised by routine or scheduled events. The plan of the day (or POD) is a great source of information that gets read to the division at morning quarters, but no one really listens, and most Divos pay no attention to it. Make sure you and your folks are aware of and up-to-date on what is going on and can react appropriately when things change. This also applies in the grander sense to inspections, assist visits, and certifications. Be prepared; do not be surprised by scheduled events.

The first time you do something should not be the first time you do something. Practice everything. Training is the key to success. Naval Special Warfare instructors always say that in times of crisis, no one rises to the occasion; they all fall back on their training. Another thing that I think originated from (or was made popular by) the Special Operators is the saying, "Slow is smooth, smooth is fast." Take your time and be deliberate; everything will proceed in a timely manner. If you rush things, you will rush to failure.

With regards to the previous paragraph, though, we want to be left-leaning. This is not a political statement; getting left of something or being left-leaning means planning ahead. Left-leaning folks are always looking and planning ahead but staying rooted in the present so as to not lose operational situational awareness. This mindset, or posturing, allows you to be efficient in your actions. If something doesn't mesh with what is planned, it probably doesn't need to happen, at least in that moment.

17

Designated Driver

Always have a plan: good, solid advice.

When I transferred to my second ship, I met the ship while it was deployed. So many of the things you would normally do when arriving at a new duty station overseas, like Japan, I just didn't do. We were only going to be back in Yokosuka for a few months before heading out for another deployment, and those months in port were scheduled to be very busy. I was scheduled to take the Inter-Cultural Relations (ICR) Course (where you learn all about living in Japan), but between the fact that we only had a short time in port and that I still had a couple of weeks before the course started, I just carried on with business as usual. I took turns driving back and forth from the base in Yokosuka to our house over on Sagami Wan. I was a pretty good driver. So good, in fact, I figured I would easily pass the driving course and get my Japanese license that was originally scheduled for after the completion of the ICR course.

As always, when you are closing in on a holiday weekend, the week flies by. It was a Wednesday, the day before

Thanksgiving, and we were on the cusp of a ninety-six-hour liberty. So, my roommates and I decided to make a run up to Tokyo and go clubbing in Roppongi, the legendary club district. The guys who routinely went there to party and meet all the expat models became known as Roppongi Warriors—I was a warrior. For this run, I volunteered to be the designated driver and drive my roommate's car—great plan, right? By the time we made it up to Tokyo, it was around 21:00—too early for clubs but not too early for a pub. True to my tasking, I stuck to sodas and water. When we finally made it to the clubs, it was around 01:00, and I shifted to coffee. We had a blast, and I was everyone's wingman.

By the time we left the clubs and made it back to the car, it was around 04:30. The guys were feeling no pain, and we swung by McDonalds (or, as the Japanese say, Mac-a-don-a-do) and grabbed a few burgers for the road. Everyone immediately passed out in a food/booze coma. I was both tired and wired, but now I had a couple of cheeseburgers and another cup of coffee in my stomach—good to go, right?

As we drove through the center of Yokohama, about halfway to Yokosuka, the sun was coming up, but the roads were still relatively empty. I approached an intersection, and the light changed from green to yellow as I went through. Unfortunately, a delivery van came through the light from my left at the same time, and I slammed on the brakes. I T-boned the van almost dead center. Luckily, I wasn't going very fast, but the van was. The damage to our car was minimal and superficial, but the van's side was dented in, and the driver hit a curb and then a bridge piling after careening off to the left. No one was hurt in our car, and the driver got out of his van and looked at the damage to his vehicle. My stomach fell into my pants—this wasn't my car, I had no insurance, and I had no license. I was in big trouble. Great call being the designated driver.

The Japanese police showed up first, and no one spoke English. About thirty minutes later, shore patrol showed up along with base police and an interpreter. The base police told me not to talk to anyone but them while there. They took my statement, and I waited.

While I was standing there, this Japanese gentleman came up to me and started talking to me, and I was guessing that he was asking me questions. On the advice of the base police, I just shrugged my shoulders and walked back to the car. Soon thereafter, the Japanese and base police came up to me and told me we were free to go and that the base legal would be in contact soon. I was not necessarily the cause of the accident, but there were some irregularities. They told me to make myself available and report immediately to my command.

When we got home, I called the XO, and he wished me a happy Thanksgiving and said he would let the CO know. He also said we'd handle it on Monday. I spent the rest of the weekend worrying about Monday.

On Monday, I reported straightaway to the CO. However, the XO had not gotten to him yet. Oops.

Surprisingly, the CO was not mad. But he was not happy either. We did not fly a Unit SITREP (Situation Report—that notifies the chain of command of an incident), but I think the CO did call the Commodore. No big deal . . .?

I finally made the time to go to the ICR class and did get my driver's license along with insurance. I did have to go back up to Yokohama and meet with the local police with an interpreter.

While the accident wasn't going to be entirely my fault, I was to be charged with driving without a license, driving without insurance, and reckless driving. I was screwed—this amounted to jail time.

I had to go up to Yokohama with an interpreter to talk with the owner of the van. It turns out the van belonged to a delivery company, and the driver claimed he was hurt. I had to present myself to the owner of the company and offer a *gomen nasai*, or official apology. But remember, this was not my fault—but in Japan, everything is the Americans' fault. And to a certain extent, I did screw up. I found out on the drive over that the man trying to talk to me at the scene was the owner of the company—the man I was going to meet with—and he was really mad. I had disrespected him at the scene, but I had no idea he was the owner. Oh man . . .

I wore my service dress blues for this meeting. As a LTjg, I was not the most bemedaled man, but I did have two rows of ribbons and medals. I didn't think I was that impressive. I purchased a gift set of whiskey at the Navy Exchange—Johnnie Walker Blue with two crystal tumblers and a large box of chocolates. I also had an envelope with about five thousand yen (about one thousand USD) to offer in compensation for the injured employee. This was going to be expensive.

When we arrived, we expected to meet the owner and the injured employee, as well as the owner's assistant/interpreter. The owner and his assistant were there, but not the employee. The owner, who I'll call Sakuta-san, had a very sour look on his face. I offered a very deep bow (as advised by the interpreter) and maintained a posture that put my head below the owner's. We stood across from each other over a low table between two couches. I first offered the chocolates, which he accepted with a curt nod, and then the whiskey, which got a more favorable response. I then offered the envelope with another deep bow and a quiet, "Sakuta-san, *gomen nasai, gomen nasai, gomen nasai.*" With each *gomen nasai*, I bowed slightly deeper. Sakuta-san's face reddened. I thought I was about to get blasted. But he offered me a seat, pulled my interpreter to the side, and began rapidly talking with him.

When they were finished, Sakuta-san and my interpreter sat down and said that Sakuta-san was very embarrassed. First, he did not realize how much of an important man I was (the SDBs did the trick!). Second, he greatly appreciated the grade of whiskey. And third, and most important, his employee failed to show up for the meeting. This was a big deal to Sakuta-san. I told the interpreter to relay to Sakuta-san that I was not that important, only the navigator and a very junior officer, that I am glad he will enjoy the whiskey, and even though the employee was not there, this was not a waste of time, and that I was humbled and pleased to meet the owner of the company. I further asked him to express my deep shame and embarrassment for not talking to him at the scene because I was advised not to by the U.S. Navy Police, and I just did not know who he was. The interpreter passed this message along with the utmost sincerity.

Sakuta-san considered this for a few moments, grunted a "*so desu,*" and looked up at me. He then said something to the interpreter, who told me that Sakuta-san wanted to know everything about the accident. I told him everything. Everything about the night in Roppongi, my decision to be the designated driver even though I had no license or insurance, about driving back, about the accident, about my command, about the police, and about the charges I was to own up to.

We met eyes; I lowered my head slightly, and he pushed the envelope back across the table to me. He looked at the interpreter and said, "You drive, we drink." He then cracked the bottle of Johnnie Walker Blue and poured us both three fingers into the gift set tumblers. I thought to myself, *What just happened?*

Over the next hour or so, we ate chocolate, drank whiskey, and became friends. What happened was because of honesty, accountability, a respect for culture, and sincere respect between men. Also, a TON of luck.

It turns out that Sakuta-san's employee stopped communicating with him, and he believed that the employee was lying about the injury. The man was fired the next day. Sakuta-san had been in the Japanese Navy as an enlisted man, and being the navigator of the ship was indeed important. He appreciated my honesty and took my account of what happened that morning over the word of his employee. He recognized that I was only following orders when I did not talk to him. He was also humbled by my show of respect for him and his culture. Also, it turned out that he was school chums with the Chief Magistrate of Yokohama and intended on getting all my charges dropped.

The takeaway here is that, while stationed overseas, you may feel like you live there, but you are still a guest. Respect the culture and get to learn some of the intricacies. I learned more over those couple of hours with Sakuta-san than I ever did in a classroom. But because of my actions, I ended up taking a masters course when the ICR would have more than sufficed. In every country, there are reasons the rules exist, and it is important that you pay attention to them all. I made great friends with Sakuta-san, and we traded holiday cards until he passed in the late 1990s. The other takeaway comes down to being honest. Oh, and having a little bit of luck didn't hurt either.

Keeping these lessons in mind, the story doesn't end there.

When we got back to Yokosuka, the interpreter and I went to my CO and reported what happened. It appeared we were on a good trajectory.

I appeared in Japanese court a few weeks later, before Sakuta-san's buddy. I remember the room being low-lit and tan, with a black runner around the ceiling. The floor was a tatami mat, and I had to remove my shoes. I approached the dais where the magistrate sat and presented myself to him along with my driving and insurance credentials. He looked at me and said two of the three charges had been dropped, and I was to be convicted of driving without a license: a $1,000 fine and no jail. Yes! When I called down to Navy Legal in Yokosuka, I thought I was home-free. I had to pay my fine the next month, just before we deployed. I had it all figured out. I could finally relax after three months of anxiety. I spent the rest of the weekend in Tokyo on liberty and had a great time.

What I didn't know was that the minute they hung up the phone with me, Legal released a message that put me on international legal hold, which meant I could not leave the country until I paid my fine. That ignited a shitstorm at 16:30 on a Friday afternoon. And remember, this was before cell phones—no one could get ahold of me until Monday morning, when I caught the train back down to Yokosuka.

To say my CO was in a furious panic is a little bit of an

overstatement, but whatever is just short of panic is where he was—and pissed. When I crossed the quarterdeck, the OOD said, "CO is looking for you and told me that you were to report directly to him when you arrived." I shrugged my shoulders and went right up to his cabin. Upon arrival, I got flame-sprayed by both him and the XO, who were waiting for me. In between "fucks" and "goddamns," I heard, "International legal hold," "a ship can't deploy without its Navigator," and a lot more "goddamns" and "fucks."

I put my hands up in protest and said, "Whoa, whoa, whoa, gents, I've got this! This is no problem. I just pay my fine, and I am done."

They looked at me and asked, "Don't you know you are on international legal hold?"

I replied, "What?" So we called Legal who said that the minute I paid my fine, I was off legal hold.

The CO said, "You are expected in the Commodore's office in one hour and in the Cave at 13:00."

I asked, "The Cave?"

"Yes," the CO replied. "The Cave, Seventh Fleet, wants to see you. Oh, neither actually knew about your accident until this weekend. Good luck."

When I met with the Commodore, I explained what happened, and I got off with, "You are one lucky bastard, Nav." I didn't really feel lucky—it was a ton of self-inflicted stress that cost me almost two thousand dollars when all was said and done, and I still had to go and see Seventh Fleet.

The commander of the U.S. Seventh Fleet at that time was, to me, a guy you would follow into combat anytime, anywhere. I really liked and respected him. This was another man I did not want to disappoint. When I got to his office, I stepped up to his desk and reported, "Admiral, LTjg Nilsson, reporting as ordered, sir."

He looked up and said, "Nilsson, what the fuck?"

I offered a feeble, "Well, sir, see . . ." and spilled my guts. I stood at attention for about twenty minutes and told my story. He did not interrupt me once.

When I was finished, he said, "Your fine is a thousand bucks? That's it? And then you are free to go?"

I replied, "Yes, sir."

He then kind of grinned at me and said, "Well, okay, then. See you on deployment, Nav." And I left.

The author and Commander, Seventh Fleet on deployment, 1997

A couple of takeaways from this story and a postscript: Genuinely, always go out with a plan, but make sure it is a good plan with all your bases considered. Be honest and forthright with your bosses, especially when you screw up. As for the postscript—back in the day, the ICR was completely voluntary, a highly recommended course, but not required. After my shenanigans, the ICR course was made mandatory for not only service members but also dependents, and the driving course is incorporated into the ICR course.

18

Best Practices

There are a number of things that I consider to be "best practices" that are applicable to junior officers and, frankly, senior officers as well. You might think that some of these things are simply intuitive or second nature, but for many, they are not. Here are a few of my best practices:

- Ensure your plan is well-known and everyone knows your expectations. Clear and unambiguous direction is required. A good plan creates unity, but when it becomes necessary to diverge from the plan, everyone should also know exactly what they need to do to get back on track.
- Study and understand doctrine and tactics. Doctrine and tactics are the foundation for creative thought that enables a new approach to a unique situation.

- Recognize that the current training environment might not support your projected operational environment; you need to aggressively pursue and create training opportunities to prepare your team for combat.
- Understand how to fight on the thin line—in other words, with minimal communications. Understand the mission intent (commander's intent) and execute.
- Do not be indecisive in public—make your decision. Waffle with your LCPO and LPO behind closed doors. Listen and take heed of their council, but in the end, the decision is yours.
- Cleanliness. Make it your daily mission to keep your spaces clean. Why? Why do we harp on cleanliness? I can give you three reasons why this is a priority for you and your Sailors:

  1. You can immediately identify what is leaking, broken, or out of place.
  2. You establish a pleasant working environment, which is easier to maintain than doing cheetah flips to clean it up after it becomes a disaster.
  3. Pride in ownership of a space.

- Find a hobby. Do something that has nothing to do with the Navy. I had a buddy who played the guitar as a hobby. He was really good and played at parties, small get-togethers, and while we were on deployment. You need a mental escape. I like to read and do PT. I do both way better than I play the guitar.

- PT. At VMI, PT is a way of life. Keep it up. It is good for your sanity and blood pressure, and you are still required to do it. I can still out-PT two-thirds of my commands. It is okay to blow off some steam playing Xbox (I even had one as Chief of Staff of a strike group), but don't let it become your only outlet.
- Read everything. Fiction, nonfiction, tactics, doctrine, tech manuals, CO's standing orders and battle orders, etc. Reading expands your knowledge base and your vocabulary.

LTjg Nilsson, Underway in Stateroom, South China Sea, 1997

- Bridge watch. Earlier, I mentioned the OODA loop. While I could write a book on this topic (and there are already really good ones out there that you should read), I want to both reiterate and develop this a little more because it is worth repeating. Develop a cycle on the bridge. I would constantly move. Centerline pelorus to the radar, to the starboard bridgewing (take a look behind you), back to the radar, to the port bridgewing (take a look behind you), and back to the centerline pelorus. Talk to your watch standers (to include the aft lookout), use your binoculars, and keep CIC engaged. The point is: move, look, engage, and do not anchor yourself in one spot. The Mark 1 eyeballs are the best tools you have. And listen to your gut. If it looks and feels wrong, it probably is—use your tools!

- Collateral duties. You will hear that the term Navy is actually an acronym—Never Again Volunteer Yourself. Dismiss that notion outright. There are so many opportunities out there; you just have to seek them out. Collateral duties tend to be approached as the bane of many a Division Officers' existence, but if you get ahead of the curve and volunteer for the ones you want to do and the ones that interest you, they can really help round out your development. For example, collateral duties such as VBSS boarding officer and surface search and rescue swimmer can be challenging and fun. If you are a closet accountant, a wardroom mess treasurer might be right up your alley (and usually something no one else wants to do). If you really enjoy photography, writing, or both, a collateral duty public affairs officer (PAO) will get you access and opportunities to see and do things you might not normally be a part of. Or, the morale, welfare, and recreation officer will get you tied into lots of opportunities, and you will become the expert on what there is to do when you pull into port (aside from drinking and finding the nearest Wi-Fi signal). These should be approached as opportunities rather than duties. Plus, collateral duties will force you to interact with your chain of command on a much more routine basis and outside the scope of just your job. In short, collateral duties can be very rewarding.

- Listen to your Chiefs.

19

Whiteboard'isms

These were out-of-context statements that I would write up on the whiteboard in my office or stateroom. They would always be centered at the top of the board. I would write these statements or phrases out of context to make everyone think. I wanted my subordinates to think about why I put it up there—did they mess up, did we miss something, was something coming up that I wanted them to be wary of, and what was the context? Usually, the phrase was prompted by something—not always bad, but it was a theme I wanted the leadership to be thinking of. For you, as a junior officer, these are things or "thought bubbles" for you to just think about: what they might mean to you and how they might enter your day-to-day.

- Know what "right" looks like
- Forceful watch team backup
- Procedural compliance
- Supervision
- Professional curiosity

- No artificial pressures
- Good leaders must also be good followers
- We are not as good as our reputation
- We are not as good as we think we are
- DYFJ (Do Your "Fun" Job)
- Anyone can be replaced, even me
- If you are not going to help, please step back and stop stealing my oxygen
- We facilitate success
- We work for our subordinate commands, not the other way around
- Don't be afraid or too proud to ask for advice or help

20

Your Philosophy

When I went through the PXO pipeline for the first time, we had to attend the Command Leadership School. It was a "gentleman's course," meaning no tests or graded work. It was the first time I had attended a Navy school that was set up like that. One of the things that we did have, though, was homework: reading, writing, and thinking. One of our assignments was to come up with a command vision and philosophy. I thought, I am going to be the XO, not the CO—it is my job to execute the CO's vision and philosophy; why bother with this? I also found out that ADM Nimitz never had one, and he did okay. I was being lazy and didn't put any effort into making one.

When I sat my Command at Sea Board a couple of years later, it bit me in the ass. I didn't think I'd be asked to come up with one on the spot, but they asked. I came up with: "Work hard, play hard." I thought I was able to BS the board, but they saw right through it and called me on it during the debrief. I passed, but they said, "Get a philosophy."

As a Division Officer, you don't necessarily need one, but

119

you should have a vision for your division and how you expect to run things—and they should know your expectations as well. More importantly, you need to read and understand your CO's vision and philosophy. For many of us, it is a road map to how we operate and what we expect not only from our subordinates but also from ourselves.

Below was my last command vision, philosophy, mission, and principles statement. It didn't change much over four command tours. It fits on one piece of paper, is simple, and is to the point.

CNBG 2 Vision, Philosophy, Mission, and Principles

Vision

As the Immediate Superior in Command (ISIC) for the NBG-2 Units, we will work tirelessly to facilitate their success, advocate for their requirements, and provide leadership, oversight, and guidance to ensure the highest state of combat readiness and mission accomplishment across the spectrum of warfare.

NBG-2 and its elements will always be ready, trained, and agile to meet the full range of a combatant commander's contingencies, from major combat operations to humanitarian assistance and disaster relief.

Philosophy

The operational mission of the Naval Beach Group requires it and its elements to operate offensively in a high-density, multi-threat environment as an integral member of an amphibious task force or expeditionary strike group and the U.S. Marine Corps. Our overarching mission is to furnish combat-ready, fully manned, trained, and equipped amphibious elements to the operational commanders that form the Navy Support Element detachment, and provide similar services during all forms of amphibious logistics operations. To facilitate this success, we shall:

Train to lethality. We will oversee the training and certification of the NBG Detachments and our reserve components to effectively deploy; and conduct the Amphibious Warfare (AMW) certifications for the ships. Attentive to doctrine, training is the foundation for effective and efficient combat operations. We will realistically train and evaluate, and be harder on ourselves than any outside evaluator. A lack of training results in unskilled, unsafe, and timid operators—training is the key to developing bold, confident, creative, and lethal warfighters.

Safety in operations. We will infuse safety into every aspect of our lives; our Operational Risk Management (ORM) must be well-thought-out, and must be understood by all. ORM is a dynamic process that must be reevaluated as evolutions or operations progress. I will not tolerate safety or procedural violations; our operations are dangerous and violating standards is self-defeating. Safe training is effective training; effective training primes safe operations.

Support to the warfighters. We will provide administrative, materiel, and logistic support for our home guard and deployed forces, and endeavor to forecast and get ahead of their requirements through advocacy and engagement. Naval Beach Group equipment is complex and highly capable, but if it does not work, we cannot do our jobs; we will ensure our units have what they need to maintain their tools of the trade, and maintain the monopoly of violence.

Support innovation. We will provide support to various research and development organizations for fleet-directed evolutions, and innovate efficiency, effective lethality, and maneuver in amphibious warfare.

Principles

Honesty and trust. I do not lie, cheat, or steal, nor do I tolerate those who do. I expect the same from you. We are a combat team and must trust and respect each other as Sailors and as fellow human beings. We are a professional organization and will act like it at all times—professional relationships build trust. I will always let you know what I know and when I can, the "why" behind it; when I cannot, rest assured that I will make decisions in the best interests of the command and the Group. I trust you to do your job—so do it.

Ambassadorship. We will always make our Navy and our Nation proud through our behavior, stewardship, and goodwill. Remember who you represent; be loyal to the Country, the Navy, the Beach Group, and each other.

Do your best. Set your personal standards high, and grow professionally and personally. Never settle for the minimum, and if you spot a deficiency, fix it or propose a solution. No one joined this fighting force to fail.

As the vanguard of any amphibious operation, we will lead from the front with moral courage, a clear sense of duty, and tradition-born valor in action, in both peace and war.

HONOR - COURAGE - COMMITMENT

21

Learning Is a
Never-Ending Process

This little book is geared for junior officers with an eye on surviving (and excelling) the first few years and building a career based on a foundation of common sense, excellence, and professionalism. Life changes for officers at the mid-grade level. The Navy has multiple off-ramps you can take, but if you decide to stay the course, it gets really interesting and really fun.

I had two years as XO of a DDG and excelled at it; a literal bump knocked me off the traditional path and put me on the special mission path. When I took over as Executive Officer of Beachmaster Unit ONE in Coronado, California, I had no idea what I was doing operationally. One afternoon, one of my OICs, a CWO4, came into my office and asked what I wanted to do about a certain event. I had no idea what he wanted, but I had to make a decision.

At that point, I said to him, "Bos'n, I have no idea what you are talking about. Educate me." Without a word, he turned and walked out of my office. About ten minutes later, he came back in with a stack of pubs, tech manuals, and instructions and dropped this four-foot stack on my desk.

He said to me, "XO, here is your education." He then said, with his Texas drawl, "Sir, what we do is unique; nobody really understands what we do. For you to be our advocate, you need to be the smartest motherfucker in the room. Right now, I am the smartest motherfucker in the room. For us to have a conversation, I need you to be the smartest motherfucker."

I love my Bos'ns. Deck Warrants and LDOs have the toughest jobs in the Navy. They train and motivate Sailors to do the jobs no one really wants to do and do them willingly. I have found that, by and large, they tend to be the best leaders. In order for me to lead these experts, I needed to become the smartest motherfucker in the room. So I did.

It is never too late to learn. It is never too late to grow. It is never too late to recognize your shortcomings and overcome them. Even as an O-6, I still learn from the experts around me every day.

22

A Generational Perspective

I recognized as I edged closer and closer to retirement that the Navy I was in was no longer MY Navy—it had become yours. This recognition or realization reminded me of a discussion I had with some Ensigns a few years ago. We were talking about the SWO culture, what it meant to be an SWO, and what they'd heard during their short time on the waterfront. Words and phrases were tossed around like stickler, eat-their-young, dorks, fallen angels, or nuke waste. Like most monikers, there is some truth in all of it. But I offered to them and challenged them that the culture they wanted the SWO community to be was in their hands—they had both the power and responsibility to make the SWO community as cool and desirable as they wanted to. It was their turn; my time was done.

I also recognize that while I offer advice and a perspective on leadership, things are different now. As junior officers, you are closer in age and interest to your Sailors than you are to your leadership. Your perspective is a critical component of leaders and leadership, and we should listen.

Your leaders are of a different generation of Sailors than you are; you need to recognize that. We are old sea dogs, and sometimes we have a hard time learning new tricks. However, and just as important, we as senior leaders need to recognize that our style of leadership needs to adapt to the people we are leading if we want to get the most out of you. I always expected and appreciated frank and open discussions with my junior Sailors and officers. They helped me frame my approach and my perspective. A person's perspective is a person's reality—right or wrong. I have a perspective and a perception of you and your generation, and you have a perspective and a perception of mine. Only frank and open lines of communication will make sure we do not find ourselves at odds.

I owe it to you to learn and understand what motivates you. You owe it to me to consider my responsibility as a commanding officer. At the foundation of this remains the requirement to complete the mission, and you have to trust in the leadership's ability to do it.

We are at a particularly challenging time in our nation's history. I came of age when the specter of war loomed ever-present: the Cold War. The Soviet threat was just over the Fulda Gap and about to come across the North Atlantic. You were born into a decades-long hot war, the Global War on Terrorism (GWOT). The fact that you chose this profession speaks volumes about you and your generation, and I am immensely proud of you and would give just about anything to serve alongside you.

The GWOT is, for the most part, over (but there will always be terrorism), and we are refocusing on an age of great power competition. You will prepare for the war we never had. You will begin to study the adversary who has been preparing to fight you for decades. You are smarter, more agile, and more adaptive—that is your strength. You know that you are smarter, more agile, and more adaptive—and that is your weakness, because it can lead to overconfidence. Never underestimate your adversary.

I want to make something very clear. You chose to be in the profession of arms. Your job is to violently, quickly, and efficiently kill the enemy before they kill you. You are to break their will to fight, you are to break their stuff that they fight with, and you are to vanquish them from the sea and field. Everything you do in this job is geared toward this end—victory at sea and ashore. If you are not comfortable with that, find another job—you are not needed in our Navy.

So, we circle back to the fundamental art of leadership. How do I facilitate your success? Because your success enables my success. How do I convince you to do something you might not want to do and do it willingly?

I offer you the set of tools we talked about in the beginning. Tools to lead and tools to manage. Each time you use a tool, you learn more about it, you become better with it, and your work becomes a craft. No one becomes a master of their craft overnight; it takes effort and dedication. You made the choice to enter this profession, and for that, you are commended, so never stop seeking ways to improve your craft.

VMI Cadet Nilsson   *CAPT Nilsson, USN*

About the Author

CAPT Erik Nilsson, USN (Ret.) is a 1993 graduate of the Virginia Military Institute and was a recipient of the Brian Undercoffer Award for creative writing. He spent thirty years on active duty in the U.S. Navy, serving globally on amphibious ships, frigates, and destroyers; serving on an Italian amphibious squadron staff, a U.S. destroyer squadron staff, a joint staff, carrier strike group, and fleet staffs; and completing four successful command tours. Since retiring from the Navy, Nilsson is easing into the civilian workplace as a defense contractor.

Barrack Room 315/115 Graduation Celebration, 2023